Martin

Jesus Our Servant

REFLECTIONS ON THE SUNDAY READINGS
FOR MARK'S YEAR

the columba press

First published in 2008 by
the columba press
55A Spruce Avenue, Stillorgan Industrial Park,
Blackrock, Co Dublin

Cover by Bill Bolger
Origination by The Columba Press
Printed in Ireland by ColourBooks Ltd, Dublin

ISBN 978-1-85607-632-6

Table of Contents

Introduction

The Gospel of Mark

The earliest association of the shortest gospel with someone called Mark comes from Papias, who was bishop of Hierapolis in Asia Minor in the early second century. Eusebius, a church historian of the fourth century, quotes Papias as follows: 'And this is what the elder said: "When Mark became Peter's interpreter, he wrote down carefully, but not in order, as much as he remembered of the Lord's words and deeds; for he had not heard the Lord nor been one of his followers, but later, as I said, one of Peter's".' Although Papias lived in the early second century, he claims to be citing the tradition of an earlier witness from the first century. According to Papias, Mark was not an eyewitness but had access to the tradition about Jesus through Peter. If Papias' testimony is reliable, Mark was able to draw on a memory of Peter's witness for some of his work. Writing only forty years after the original event of Jesus' ministry, it is reasonable to assume that Mark had contact with several eyewitnesses. Irenaeus, in the middle of the second century, writes: 'After their (i.e. Peter and Paul's) departure, Mark, the disciple and interpreter of Peter, transmitted his preaching to us in written form.' In the late second century, Clement of Alexandria states that Mark wrote his gospel in the city of Rome. Many scholars accept the reliability of this early tradition that links the gospel of Mark to Peter and to Rome. However, the evidence is not conclusive. Some scholars prefer to locate the community behind the gospel in Syria, specifically in the city of Antioch.

Some scholars hold that the gospel of Mark was written shortly after the destruction of the Jewish temple in Jerusalem in the year 70. Several passages in the gospel may suggest that Mark and his readers were very aware of this highly significant event, which brought the Jewish revolt against Rome (66-70) to an end. Others are of the view that Mark's gospel shows little awareness of the fall of Jerusalem in the year 70 and is better dated to the closing years of the decade of the 60s. The years prior to 70 were very disturbed ones in Rome, especially for

Christians. Peter, along with Paul and other prominent believers, had been martyred in Rome during the persecution initiated
by Nero in 64CE. The emperor Nero had blamed the Christians
for the great fire that engulfed much of Rome in July 64.
Furthermore, after the death of Nero in 68, there was a period of
great instability in Rome, with no less than three emperors within
the space of a year. If Mark's gospel was written in Rome around
the year 70, it was addressed to a community that had recently
passed through a painful experience of persecution, resulting in
the loss of some of their most prominent members. This might
explain why Mark's gospel has such a strong focus on the way of
the cross to be travelled both by Jesus and his disciples.

The gospel was written for believers whose background was
predominantly pagan rather than Jewish (Gentile Christians).
The evangelist finds it necessary to explain Jewish customs to
his readers (7:3-4). Yet, Mark can take it for granted that his
readers are also familiar with the Jewish scriptures (1:2). A
Gentile Christian community with deep Jewish roots would fit
both the church of Rome and the church of Antioch.

The Acts of the Apostles refers to a 'John whose other name
was Mark' (12:12) and whose house in Jerusalem was a gather-
ing place for the first disciples. He was clearly a Jewish Christian
and he went on to become a co-worker and travelling companion of Paul for a short time (12:25; 15:37, 39). Reference is also
made to 'Mark' in three letters associated with Paul (Phm 24; Col
4:10; 2 Tim 4:11) and in the conclusion of the first letter of Peter
(1 Pet 5:13). Whether or not these references to 'Mark' refer to
one and the same person cannot be determined with certainty. If
they do refer to one and the same person, there is no conclusive
evidence to identify the evangelist with this 'Mark'.

What kind of gospel did Mark the evangelist write? One way
of exploring the overall shape of Mark's story of Jesus is by
noticing the various locations that are referred to in the course of
the gospel. Mark begins 'in the wilderness' where John was bap-
tising, and where Jesus, having been baptised by John, was
tempted (1:1-13). These opening thirteen verses can be understood as the Prologue to the gospel. If location is taken as a
guide, three main sections of Mark's gospel can be identified in
the remainder of the gospel. In 1:14 Jesus enters Galilee where

he remains for the following eight chapters. A significant shift occurs in 8:27. Here we have the first mention of the phrase 'on the way' which is repeated over the following two chapters and occurs for the last time in 10:52. In this section of the gospel (8:27-10:52) Jesus is 'on the way' to the city of Jerusalem where he will undergo his passion and death. The location presupposed by these chapters is a way between places, rather than a place in itself. In 11:1 Jesus reaches Jerusalem, and the following chapters are an account of his brief ministry in Jerusalem, culminating in his passion and death (11:1-13:37; 14:1-15:47). Corresponding to the Prologue at the beginning of the gospel, the last eight verses can be considered an Epilogue (16:1-8). The gospel that begins in the wilderness concludes in an empty tomb. In the Judean wilderness, which is a place of death, John the Baptist makes a promise of new life (1:7-8). At the tomb, another place of death, a young man makes an announcement of new life (16:6-7). The emergence of new life in the wilderness is an underlying theme of Mark's gospel. The majority of scholars are agreed that Mark's gospel originally ended at 16:8 with the finding of the empty tomb. Some of the early scribes who subsequently copied the manuscript of Mark's gospel added an account of various appearances of the risen Lord to the disciples, thereby bringing the ending of Mark's gospel into line with the endings of the other gospels.

There are a number of distinctive characteristics of Mark's gospel. The evangelist tells his story of Jesus with an unusual urgency. The little word 'immediately' occurs forty-two times in the gospel and eleven times in the first chapter alone. Jesus in Mark's gospel appears to be in a great hurry. Mark also emphasises the deeds of Jesus over his words. Jesus' ministry in Mark consists principally of action. There is less of the content of Jesus' teaching in Mark than in any other gospel. His gospel also offers the most human portrait of Jesus. Like any human being, Jesus becomes tired (6:31) and hungry (11:12). He feels a wide range of human emotions including pity (1:41), anger (3:1), wonder (6:6), compassion (6:34), indignation (10:14), and love (10:21). Jesus does not know everything (13:32) and his power is sometimes limited (6:5). Matthew and Luke – and especially John - give us a more exalted picture of Jesus. Yet, Mark is aware

7

that Jesus, while being fully human, has a unique relationship with God. The most important title given to Jesus in Mark's gospel is 'Son of God'. For Mark, it is above all the death of Jesus that reveals what it means to say that Jesus is the Son of God. His death expresses his faithfulness to God and to all of God's people.

In his portrait of Jesus' disciples Mark highlights their failure to a greater extent than the other evangelists. Matthew and Luke tend to soften Mark's uncompromising portrayal of Jesus' disciples. Mark's sobering portrait of the disciples may have served a pastoral purpose. He was writing to a community that had recently come through an experience of persecution. Many in the community may have weakened under pressure, and, at the time Mark wrote his gospel, they may have been trying to come to terms with their own failure to confess Jesus publicly. They probably identified with the seed which fell on rocky soil in the parable of the sower – those who 'endure only for a while; then when trouble or persecution arises on account of the word, immediately they fall away' (4:17). Mark's portrait of Jesus' disciples would have been a reassuring word for them. Even the first disciples, in whom Jesus had invested so much time and energy, failed spectacularly. Yet, Jesus was faithful to them. Mark wanted to assure his community that they too would experience the Lord's faithfulness, in spite of past failures.

The Season of Advent

First Sunday of Advent

The Season of Advent falls in the darkest time of the year, when the days are coming towards their shortest. As the light begins to diminish towards its weakest point, we find ourselves looking forward to the days when the light begins to increase again. Advent is very much a season which invites us to touch into our deeper longings, the yearnings for life, light, love, truth and joy. These deep yearnings are, ultimately, a longing for God. St Augustine said that our hearts are restless until they rest in God.

The first reading of the first Sunday of Advent gives expression to this deeper longer in our hearts for God; it is the heartfelt cry of God's people for a deeper relationship with God, 'Oh that you would tear the heavens and come down.' They acknowledge that there is a lack in their lives that only God can fill and, so, making use of an autumn/winter image, they cry out, 'We have all withered like leaves and our sins blew us away like the wind.' It is as if they are crying out in the winter of their spirit for God's coming. They know they have not been living as God intended them to live; much of what was good in them has withered. Yet, they also know that God remains faithful to them and can renew them. Like the potter, God can make something new out of the mess of their lives.

This is the frame of mind and heart in which we too are invited to begin Advent. We begin Advent acknowledging the winter of our own spirit, recognising that in ways we have become like withered leaves blown about by the wind. More importantly, we begin Advent in the conviction that God is constantly coming towards us as one who can change us for the better. We begin Advent, calling on God the potter to remake us, so that we can shine forth more clearly as the work of his hands. In that sense, Advent is a hopeful season, because it is a time when we celebrate the good news that God's coming will respond to the winter of our spirit.

God comes to renew what God has already given to us rather than to give us what we have never received. Another image, this time from the New Testament, expresses this well. God comes to fan into a living flame the gifts that we have been given through his Son, Jesus. What St Paul says to the Corinthian church in today's second reading could be said to all of us here today: 'I never stop thanking God for all the graces you have received through Jesus Christ. I thank him that you have been enriched in so many ways.' As we begin Advent, we recognise all the ways that God has graced us through his Son. But we also acknowledge that we have allowed these gifts to die back, to wither like leaves, and so we long for God to come and fan these gifts into living flames. Advent is a time when we cry to God out of the winter of our spirit, 'Let your face shine on us and we shall be saved.' We long for the warmth and light of God's presence to bring to life whatever good has died within us. Our lighting of the Advent wreath over the next four weeks gives expression to that longing within us.

Advent is a time when we are invited to become more spirit-ually alert – alert to how we have allowed what is best in us to wither, and alert to the Lord whose fuller coming into our lives can renew and remake us. The call to be alert is the call we hear from Jesus in the gospel reading today. We know that certain forms of behaviour can work against that kind of alertness, such as excessive drinking and the misuse of drugs. We also know that other forms of behaviour can enhance the kind of alertness to ourselves and to the Lord that Jesus calls for. In particular, taking time and space for prayer in our lives will make us more spiritually alert.

Advent is a season when we might give a little more time to prayer than we would normally do. It is a prayerful, contempla-tive season, when we are invited to enter into a spirit of prayer-ful waiting, when we are called to make the simple Advent prayer an integral part of our lives, 'Come, Lord Jesus.' This prayer is the Christian version of the prayer of the people of Israel in the first reading, 'Tear the heavens and come down.' In making this prayer our own, we enter into that spirit of Advent longing and waiting which is the essence of this season.

Second Sunday of Advent

At this time of year we think about buying Christmas presents for people. We may be at the stage of asking people what they would like for Christmas. People may already have been asking us the same question, and we might have found ourselves wondering, 'What do I want for Christmas?'

This second Sunday of Advent might prompt us to ask a deeper question of ourselves, 'What does God want for me, for us, this season of Advent?' If we were to put that question to John the Baptist who appears in today's gospel reading, 'What does God want of us?', he would likely say back to us, 'Prepare a way for the Lord.' He would say to us, 'What God wants for you this Advent is that you make way for the coming of God's Son, that you receive him more fully into your lives.' That is the fundamental call of Advent, 'Receive the Lord who is coming.' That primary call of Advent is matched by the primary prayer of Advent, 'Come, Lord Jesus.' In praying that prayer, we are expressing our desire to receive the Lord more fully into our lives, to grow in our relationship with him.

Advent is a season when we are called to allow Christ to grow in us. The great saint of Advent, apart from John the Baptist, is Mary. Mary's Advent was that nine month period when Jesus physically grew within her, until she was ready to offer him to the world. Our Advent is much shorter than Mary's, four weeks in all, but it is also the time when we are called to allow Jesus to grow spiritually within us, so that we can offer him to the world by the lives that we live. The call to allow Jesus to grow within us may first be heard as a call to repent, which is the call that John the Baptist makes in today's gospel reading. To repent is to turn away from what is not of the Lord and to turn towards what is of Lord. If the Lord is to grow within us, there will always be something that we have to turn away from or let go of. Advent invites us to look at what there might be in our lives that is blocking Christ from growing in us. In the imagery of today's first reading, we might ask ourselves: 'What are the mountains that need levelling, and the valleys that need filling in, if Christ is to grow more fully within us?'

There is a lot of emphasis today on personal growth and personal development. People, quite rightly, want to live full lives. As Christians, however, we believe that we grow as persons to the extent that Christ grows within us. Jesus was both fully divine and fully human. It was because he was fully divine, a full image of God, that he was also fully human. The more Christ grows within us, the more human we become – the more we become the person that God has created us to be. The letter to the Colossians expresses this very well: 'In Christ, the whole fullness of deity dwells bodily, and you have come to fullness in him.' Advent is the season when we strive to create a space for Christ to grow within us, so that we come to our fullness in him. A good Advent question to ask is, 'Who would I like to become this Advent, so as to make Christmas special for others?'

We may be tempted to think that 'I am who I am and I am not going to become anyone else, I am not going to change.' Yet, God is always calling us to grow into his Son. God never ceases to call us to change. God is patient with us when we appear to be deaf to that call. In the words of today's second reading, God 'is being patient with you all, wanting nobody to be lost and everybody to be brought to change their ways.' God waits patiently on us to admit Christ more fully into our lives. God's waiting on us is not a passive waiting, a kind of standing back to wait and see. God's patient waiting is expressed actively. In the words of today's gospel reading, 'I am going to send my messenger before you.' God sends us messengers to help us to create space in our lives for Christ to come and grow within us. God is actively involved in helping us to prepare a way for the Lord. God's messengers, God's help, can take many and varied forms. Advent is a time to become more alert to the resources that God offers us to grow into the person of Christ.

Third Sunday of Advent

Christmas day is only two weeks away. It is a time when we joyfully celebrate the birth of Christ. Something of the joy of Christmas comes through in the prayers and readings of this third Sunday of Advent, traditionally known as Gaudete Sunday – 'Rejoice, Sunday'. In the first reading, the people of Israel exclaim: 'I exult for joy in the Lord, my soul rejoices in my God.' In the second reading, St Paul calls upon the Thessalonians: 'Be happy at all times.'

Yet, that call to joy can often fall on deaf ears in the run up to Christmas. Most people look forward to Christmas, but some people among us will dread the thought of Christmas. Those who are prone to depression can find that the prospect of Christmas only makes their depression worse. Those who have recently lost loved ones will be wondering how they will get through the first Christmas without them. People who live alone and who find life a lonely experience will know that their loneliness can be compounded by the knowledge that most people are celebrating Christmas in the company of family and friends.

Nevertheless, the call to joy in today's readings may have something to say to those who find it hard to get into joyful mood in the run-up to Christmas. Indeed, it has something to say to all of us about where true joy is to be found. When Paul calls on the Thessalonians to be happy at all times, or to rejoice always, he was well aware that life was not a bed of roses for them. We know from elsewhere in his letter that some members of the community had recently died and that there was a great deal of grief among them. Yet, to this community that was suffering affliction and loss Paul could say: 'Rejoice always.'

Having called on them to rejoice, he immediately called on them to 'pray constantly', and 'to give thanks in all circumstances'. Paul does not say, 'give thanks for all things', as some translations have it, but 'give thanks *in* all things'. Many things can happen to us and to others for which we cannot give thanks because they do not correspond to God's will for our lives. However, Paul would say that no matter what happens to us, we can always give thanks in the midst of it. We may be struggling in various ways, but as Christians we never cease giving thanks because God has blessed us in Christ. That remains the good news, even when we are suffering in one way or another.

Eucharist means thanksgiving. When we come to Mass we come to give thanks, even if the situation out of which we have come is far from satisfactory. We come to Mass to give thanks because we know that, whatever may be happening to us, in the words of Paul in today's second reading, 'God has called you and God will not fail you.' If we could take that word away with us, 'God will not fail you', and carry it into whatever difficult situation in which we may find ourselves, we will be moved to give thanks, we will find a joy welling up within us. We come to Mass to give thanks because we know that, in the words of today's gospel reading: 'There stands among you – unknown to you – the one who is coming after me.' John the Baptist announces that the Word who became flesh stands among us. Standing suggests strength. We stand when we are strong; when we are weak, we sit or lie down. The Lord stands among us in the strength of his risen life, as one whose strength supports us in our weakness. Paul can call on us to rejoice always and to give thanks in all circumstances because the Lord is always standing alongside us.

In the run up to Christmas, today's readings call on us to enter into the joy which is the fruit of our faith. That will often require a conscious effort on our part. We might decide to make it a point every day to be grateful for something good in our lives, for some way that the Lord has blessed and continues to bless us. We discover the joy of our faith especially when we live our faith, when we love each other as God has loved us in Christ. It is in giving as Christ gave that we receive, it is in serving that we find joy. In that second reading, St Paul says to the Thessalonians: 'Never try to suppress the Spirit.' The Holy Spirit within us is always calling us to serve others in some way. In responding to that call of the Spirit we discover the joy of our faith.

Fourth Sunday of Advent

The four candles of the Advent wreath are now lighting. All that remains is the white candle at the centre of the wreath, which will be lit on Christmas day. We are moving ever closer to the feast of Christmas. John the Baptist has been the main character in the gospel readings for the last two Sundays. Today, the focus is on Mary, the mother of Jesus. If John the Baptist points ahead to Jesus, Mary actually brings Jesus to us.

In today's gospel reading, she is presented as saying 'yes' to a call from God, the call to be the mother of God's Son. Her saying 'yes' did not come easily or immediately. The gospel reading states that initially she was 'disturbed' by this call, and that she then went on to question it: 'How can this be?' Eventually, she surrendered to what God wanted of her with the words: 'Let what you have said be done to me.' She stands in a long line of biblical women who faithfully served the purposes of God. Her readiness to serve God's purposes had enormous implications for us all. Because of her generous response to God's call, God's Son became flesh, and we were given the opportunity to become his followers, to take him as our way, our truth and our life.

This young woman from the insignificant village of Nazareth had enormous influence for good on all our lives because of her generous response to God's presence. We can often underestimate the extent of our own influence for good when we too, like Mary, make ourselves available to serve God's purposes. Our own 'yes' to what God may be asking of us will always benefit others. God can work powerfully through our efforts to do whatever God may be asking of us. If I am living in a way that corresponds to God's desire for my life, those with whom I am in contact will be supported in their own efforts to live as God is calling them to live. The opposite is also true. Our failure to respond to the Lord's promptings undermines others and makes their efforts to do God's will all the more difficult. We live very interdependent lives, whether we are aware of that or not. That is especially true when it comes to our relationship with God.

Responding to God's call does not come easy to us. We often have to struggle to discover what God may be asking of us, and then we may find ourselves struggling further to do what God appears to be asking of us. The gospel reading this morning suggests that Mary's 'yes' to God's call came after a period of struggle. In our first reading we find David engaged in a similar struggle. It took David some time to discover what God was asking of him. Initially, David had decided that he was going to build a magnificent house for God to dwell in. It seemed like a good idea, and the prophet Nathan supported David's plan. However, it became clear that what was in David's mind was not what was in God's mind. God did not want David to build a temple. Through the prophet Nathan, the Lord said to David: 'The Lord will make you a house.' David learned that what he wanted was not what God wanted. We are all prone to making the same mistake as David. We can confuse our plans and purposes with God's plans and purposes. As believers, we always have to be asking ourselves: 'Is this really what God is asking of me?' St Paul in today's second reading makes reference to 'the way the eternal God wants things to be'. Mary understood the way the eternal God wanted things to be, and she responded fully to what God wanted.

When it comes to the task of discovering the way that God wants things to be, and to the further task of living in accordance with that, we are not left to our own devices. The second reading this morning begins with Paul's great exclamation: 'Glory to God who is able to give you the strength to live according to the good news I preach.' The Lord works with us to help us to live lives that correspond to his purposes for ourselves and for others. In the run up to Christmas, we might ask the Lord to help us to discern what he may be asking of us over the Christmas period and to give us the strength to do what he may be asking of us. If our living of Christmas corresponds to God's purpose for our lives, it will be a happier and a more blessed Christmas for those whose lives we influence.

Christmas: Midnight Mass

Children have a wonderful way of entering into the story of the first Christmas. The nativity play captures their imagination; they play their parts with enthusiasm. It is a story that is very accessible to them. At Christmas we celebrate the good news that God has become accessible, not just to children, but to all of us. God is now revealed in a human life, in a life that began as all our lives began, as a vulnerable and helpless infant. New born children are very accessible, very engaging; they draw us towards themselves. We find ourselves getting close to them; we bring our face close to theirs and we look at them with wonder. We love to take them up in our arms and to hold them for a while. They have nothing to say to us and, yet, they communicate with us very powerfully, so powerfully that we can become oblivious to others as long as we have them in our arms.

In and through Mary and Joseph's new born child, God was communicating with us very powerfully. Matthew in his gospel names this child Emmanuel, God-with-us. There is a sense in which every new born child is Emmanuel, God-with-us. Every new born child is an image of God and reveals God the Creator. As Christians we believe that the new born child of Mary and Joseph was an image of God in a unique sense. That is why, according to Matthew's gospel, the wise men from the East worshipped this child. That is why as Christians we have been celebrating his birth every year for the last two thousand years. We celebrate this child's birth every year because we know who this child became. It is because the adult Jesus has in some way spoken to us and engaged us that we celebrate his birth every year. It is because we know that he lived and died and rose from the dead for us that his birth is so important to us. It is because we believe that this child of Mary and Joseph is, in the words of tonight's gospel reading, Saviour, Christ and Lord that we recognise his birth as good news to be celebrated.

As we return to our homes after this Mass and, hopefully, have a really enjoyable day or couple of days, it is worth remembering why we are celebrating. Our celebration can easily become a thing in itself, detached from what it is that gives rise to it. We celebrate because, in the words of the angels to the shepherds in the gospel reading, we have heard 'news of great joy, a joy to be shared by the whole people'. The good news is that God has drawn near to us in and through a human life. In doing so God has shown us what God is really like, and God has also shown us what being truly human is really like. Jesus both reveals God to us and also reveals ourselves to us. Jesus was both fully divine and fully human. We learn from him who God is and who we are called to be.

We learn this primarily from the adult Jesus rather than the child Jesus. Even though at Christmas we celebrate the feast of the child Jesus, it is really a feast, like all the Christian feasts, that calls on us to focus on the adult Jesus who lived, died and rose from the dead and who, as risen Lord, is as present to us today as the child Jesus was present to Mary and Joseph, the shepherds and wise men that first Christmas. He is present to us tonight as we gather to celebrate the Eucharist. In coming to the Eucharist we are like the shepherds in the gospel reading who hurried away from their flocks to Bethlehem to welcome and receive this gift of God that had been made known to them. The gospel reading says that, having gone to Bethlehem and found what had been told to them, they went back to their flocks glorifying and praising God for all they had heard and seen. They went back to celebrate, as we will be doing this Christmas day.

The shepherds went to Bethlehem to receive the child Jesus. We come to the Eucharist to receive the risen Lord. In receiving him in the Eucharist we are at the same time invited to receive him more fully into our lives, so that he can continue to live his life in and through our lives. That is the great Christian calling, the great Christmas calling. The Lord wants to be born anew within each one of us. He wants to live and work in us and through us. When we allow him to do so, our lives become good news for others.

Christmas: Day Mass

It is striking the efforts people make to get home for Christmas. Christmas is a feast that moves people to get back to their roots. It draws people to make contact with those who have helped to shape and form them. The feast of Christmas seems to have the power to bring us back to basics. A striking example of that was to be found among the trenches near Armentieres on Christmas Day 1914. A twenty-five year old Lieutenant wrote a letter home in which he said: 'Detachments of British and Germans formed a line and a German and British chaplain read some prayers alternately. The whole of this was done in great solemnity and reverence.' Here were sworn enemies fighting a bitter war. But, they also knew that at a much more basic level, they were fellow human beings, who had been equally graced by the birth of God's Son. The feast of that day helped those men to see each other with new eyes. They beheld each other in a new light, the light of God's love revealed in the birth of his Son. It is hard to conceive of any other Christian feast, or indeed the feast of any other religion, having that kind of power.

The feast of Christmas can touch all our lives in an equally powerful way. We are not at war with others in the way those soldiers were at war with each other. Yet, we might find ourselves coming to this feast of Christmas battered and bruised in various ways. Some of us here today may have come through, or be in the midst of, a painful experience of one kind or another. We may be embroiled in some form of conflict that leaves us drained. We may have suffered some significant loss in recent months. Some hope we cherished may not have materialised. Our health may have deteriorated. Our faith may have grown weak. We may be troubled by some wrong we did or some good we failed to do.

Wherever and however we find ourselves this Christmas, we are invited to look up, as it were, with the shepherds. We can hear as addressed to ourselves the words the shepherds heard: 'Do not be afraid. Listen, I bring you news of great joy, a joy to be shared by the whole people. Today a saviour has been born to you.' A child has been born for all of us, whoever we are, whatever situation we find ourselves in. The birth of a child is a wonderful time for any family, a time of grace. Today we celebrate a birth that has graced us all, and continues to grace us all. The child of Mary and Joseph reveals the kindness and love of God for us all. God has given us the gift of his Son and, having given this gift, God will never take it back. God's Son has become our brother, our companion on the way, becoming like us in all things but sin. God has become flesh and dwelt, and continues to dwell, among us. God's Son who dwells among us invites us to receive from his fullness, grace upon grace. In receiving from him in this way, we are empowered to rise above all that oppresses us and diminishes us. Here is a wonderful gift that calls us out of our trenches and has the potential to transform how we see ourselves and each other.

Christmas is a feast of light. It is celebrated just as the days begin to get longer. Within our own Irish tradition we have recognised this dimension of the feast of Christmas, with our custom of lighting candles and placing them in the front windows of our homes. At Christmas we celebrate the coming into the world of the true light which enlightens everyone, in the words of this morning's gospel reading. The glory of the Lord shone around the shepherds and shines around all of us. We are invited to stand under that light, the light of God's favour, and to allow that light to fill us and renew us. We are not asked to do anything to make this light shine. It is there; it is given to us. The feast of Christmas assures us that the light shines in the darkness and the darkness will not overcome it. God has graced us in a very definitive way, and God's gracious presence to us is a more fundamental reality than the darkness in which we sometimes find ourselves and, indeed, which we can help to create. This is the good news of great joy that was given to the shepherds on the first Christmas night and that is given to us this Christmas. It is this good news that is at the heart of all our Christmas celebrations.

Feast of the Holy Family

Most of us will have spent some of Christmas with family members. If that was not possible we probably will have made contact with family members over the Christmas, either by phone, or e-mail or letter. Christmas is very much a family feast. People travel in great numbers to be with their families at Christmas time. The centrality of the family at Christmas time is perhaps because, at some deep level, we are aware that at the heart of this feast of Christmas is a family, what we call the holy family, whose feast we celebrate today. When we refer to the holy family we think of Jesus, Mary and Joseph. Yet, when Joseph, Mary and Jesus spoke of the family, it is likely that they had in mind a much larger group than themselves. They would have thought of the extended family of grandparents, aunts and uncles, cousins, nephews and nieces. Luke in his gospel tells us that Mary and Elizabeth were sisters and, therefore, that Jesus and John the Baptist were cousins. Elizabeth and her husband Zechariah and their son John were part of Mary and Joseph's family, along with many others. It was within this wider family that Jesus, in the words of the gospel reading today, 'grew to maturity and was filled with wisdom'.

Today, the Feast of the Holy Family, is a good day to remember our own families of origin, the family into which we were born, within which, to varying degrees, we grew to maturity and were filled with wisdom. In remembering our families, we think not only of our parents, our brothers and sisters, but also of grandparents, aunts and uncles, cousins. We may have mixed feelings about our family. It is rare that someone is totally positive about the family into which they were born and in which they grew to maturity. None of our families were all holy or completely wholesome. They were imperfect communities because the people who composed them were not perfect. Amid all the good memories of family life, it is likely that we will also have some bad memories, some painful memories. For a minority, the memory of their family of origin will be more bad than good.

Today is a day to give thanks for all that was good in our family of origin. We give thanks for the care that nurtured us when we were too weak to take care of ourselves, for the many sacrifices that were made so that we might have better opportunities in life than earlier generations, for the sense of home that was created and that gave us a feeling of security, for the love that was free to let us go when we needed to move on, while always ready to welcome us home. Today's feast is also a good day to ask the Lord to help us to forgive what needs forgiving in our experience of family.

No matter where we are in our life-journey, whether we are still within our family of origin or whether we have long moved on from our family, the Lord continues to call us to grow 'to maturity', in the words of the gospel reading today. According to our first reading, Abraham heard 'the call to set out for a country that was the inheritance given to him'. We too are called to set out towards our heavenly inheritance. It is only in heaven that, as St Paul says, we will be fully conformed to the image of God's Son. That is the goal of our journey, our inheritance, to be conformed to the image of God's Son, to grow up into Christ.

Our families of origin can set us on the road towards that goal, that destination, but the journey continues throughout our lives. God never ceases to call us to grow up into Christ, to become more and more Christ-like, and it is never too late to heed that call, to make a new effort to travel that journey. It is a journey we travel in the power of the Spirit, because it is the Holy Spirit who shapes and moulds us into the person of Christ. The gospel reading today puts before us two elderly people who have travelled far on that journey, a man and a woman of the Spirit, Simeon and Anna. They were prayerful people, very attuned to God's presence, and the words they spoke to others were full of promise and truth. They exemplify what it means to grow old gracefully. To grow old gracefully is to grow towards becoming the Christ-like person we will be in eternity. This is the journey the Lord is constantly asking us to set out on. We pray this morning for the grace to be faithful to that calling, like Simeon and Anna.

Solemnity of Mary, Mother of God

The human face is endlessly fascinating. No two human faces are exactly the same. Our face is uniquely ours and, yet, one human face can be amazingly variable. When we look at someone's face we can tell whether they are happy or sad, calm or angry, relaxed or worried. It has been said that the eyes are the windows to the soul. Yet, the human face in its entirety is very revealing of the core of the person. From our own experience we know the power of the human face to attract us and draw us. We really need to see someone face to face to get to know them. If our only contact with people is by phone, email or letter, our sense of them as persons will be necessarily limited.

The first reading for today's feast offers us one of the loveliest prayers of blessing to be found in the Jewish scriptures: 'May the Lord bless you and keep you. May the Lord let his face shine on you and be gracious to you. May the Lord uncover his face to you and bring you peace.' The short blessing makes two references to the face of the Lord. Even though the people of Israel were very aware of the otherness and transcendence of God, they, nevertheless, spoke of God's face. The transcendent God had revealed his face to them in creation and, above all, in and through their history. God did not dwell only in darkness; the people had come to rejoice in the light of his presence. The prayer of blessing is a prayer that the people of Israel would continue to be graced by the light of God's presence, the light of God's face.

For us as Christians, the human face of Jesus is, at the same time, the face of God. In his second letter to the Corinthians, Paul makes reference to 'the light of the knowledge of the glory of God in the face of Christ' (2 Cor 4:6). In the words of the blessing in our first reading, the Lord God has uncovered his face to us in the life, death and resurrection of Jesus, his Son. If every human face is endlessly fascinating, this must be all the more true of the face of Jesus. The face of Jesus, in revealing his own core, also revealed the core of God. The first people to look upon the face of Jesus were his mother, Mary, and his father, Joseph. In looking upon the face of her new born son, Mary was looking upon the face of God in a way no human being had ever looked on God's

24

face before. It is because we believe that the face of Jesus is the face of God that we honour Mary as the mother of God, the mother of Jesus, Emmanuel, God with us in human form. We venerate Mary because she made it possible for all of us to look upon the face of her Son and, thereby, upon the face of God. We do not see Jesus as she saw him. Yet, we have wonderful access to him through the church, in particular, through the scriptures and the sacraments.

In this morning's second reading, Paul gives succinct expression to the mystery at the heart of today's feast: 'God sent his Son, born of a woman.' The Son of God was born of a woman, and that woman became the mother of God's Son or, as the church would later come to express it, the mother of God. When, 'at the appointed time', a woman became the mother of God's Son, it had enormous implications for all of us, as Paul highlights in that reading. God sent his Son, born of a woman, 'to enable us to be adopted as sons (and daughters)'. In sending his Son, God also sent 'the Spirit of his Son into our hearts'. That Spirit empowers us to share in Jesus' own relationship with God, moving us to address God as 'Abba, Father', as Jesus did. In sending his Son to be born of a woman, God made it possible for all of us to be born of God. Because we share in Jesus' own relationship with God, through the Spirit, he is our brother in the Spirit, and we are all his brothers and sisters. His mother becomes our mother. We venerate Mary not only as mother of God, but also as mother of the church.

The short sentence, 'God sent his Son, born of a woman' is brimful of meaning for all of us. There is a great deal to contemplate and appreciate here. We are invited to take our lead from Mary who, according to the gospel reading, 'treasured all these things and pondered them in her heart'.

Second Sunday after Christmas

We are familiar with the saying: 'Sticks and stones can break my bones but words will never harm me.' Like a lot of proverbial sayings, this one expresses a truth, but by no means the whole truth. We know from experience that words can be very harmful. People's reputation can be unjustly undermined because somebody else puts out a story about them. The story may have some truth in it, but it is likely to be only one of many stories that could be told about the person and, if it becomes the dominant story, an injustice is done. I remember once seeing a collection of old posters that were commonly displayed in Britain during the Second World War. One of them read, 'Careless talk costs lives.' That poster expresses a truth which applies as much to peace time as to war time. Careless talk can cost lives, not necessarily in the sense that it results in people being shot, but in the sense that it can seriously damage or even destroy a person's reputation. Careless talk can be damaging in other ways. We are all aware from our own experience how words spoken in anger can damage a relationship. Words can be either harmful or life-giving. The proverbial saying above does not seem to take seriously enough the power of language, a power that can be for good or for ill.

Today's gospel reading from the gospel of John could be understood as a hymn to the power of language, God's language. It begins: 'In the beginning was the Word.' The Word that God spoke in the beginning became flesh in the person of Jesus of Nazareth. Here was now a Word that could not only be heard, but could be seen and touched as well. The words we speak reveal who we are only to a limited extent. There is always much more to us than is revealed in our words. However, the Word God spoke in the beginning revealed God fully, and when this Word became flesh in Jesus, he became the fullest revelation of God that was possible in human form. God said all that could be humanly said about who he was in the person of his Son. To look on Jesus is to look on God. God has spoken to us in a language we can understand, the language of a human life. This Word who is Jesus is full of the life of God, radiant with the light of God. He calls on us to receive from his fullness, grace upon grace. He does not force his fullness upon people. At one point in John's gospel he turns to the twelve and asks: 'Do you also wish to go away?' Simon Peter on that occasion spoke for us all when he said, 'Lord, to whom can we go? You have the words of eternal life.' Jesus had the words of eternal life because he himself was the Word of life.

The words people speak to us do not always do us good. The words we hear from various quarters do not always leave us blessed. On the contrary, they can leave us damaged and diminished. The Word God spoke to us in his Son has greatly blessed and enriched us. St Paul recognises this in the second reading today when he sings: 'Blessed be God the Father of our Lord Jesus Christ who has blessed us with all the spiritual blessings of heaven in Christ.' Having been blessed by God's Word in this way, we are called to bless others by the words we speak, by the lives we live. We are called to keep on receiving from the fullness that is always being given to us in Christ, so that we can enrich others from that fullness. As was said of John the Baptist in today's gospel reading, we are to be witnesses who speak for the light.

Today we might give thanks for the times when we have spoken for the light, when the words we spoke gave life to someone touched by death, or brought some light into a situation of darkness. These were the times when our words had something of the quality of the Word that God spoke in the beginning and that became flesh in the person of Jesus. Parents have a wonderful opportunity to speak such words to their children, as have spouses to each other, and the unmarried to people close to them. All of us in different ways have the potential to speak words that make a difference for the better, that leave people more alive and enlightened. As we begin a new year we might resolve to speak words that have something of the life-giving quality of God's Word, the Word who became flesh and dwells among us.

The Feast of the Epiphany

Going on pilgrimage will always hold an attraction for us. The place towards which we journey will be significant for us as people of faith, whether it is Jerusalem, Rome, Lourdes or Compostela, or some place more local to us. However, there is more to a pilgrimage than the destination. There is the journey itself. We journey with other people of faith and on the way we can be greatly graced by our fellow pilgrims. The Lord is to be found not only in the place towards which we journey but also in the people with whom we journey. We make a distinction between a pilgrimage and a holiday. We can put up with certain hardships on a pilgrimage that we would not tolerate on a holiday. We expect that on any pilgrimage there will be times of struggle and also times of great joy and, even, exhilaration. Perhaps at some deep level we recognise that a pilgrimage is a microcosm of our lives. As believers we experience our life journey as a pilgrimage. We are journeying towards the Lord, while at the same time the Lord is journeying with us, in and through our companions on the way. We will have our transfiguration moments along the way, when we have a deep sense of the Lord's loving presence. We will also have our Gethsemane moments when we sense that the Lord is asking too much of us and we wonder can we keep going.

Today's readings speak to us of pilgrimage. In the first reading from the prophet Isaiah, there is a wonderful vision of the pagan nations coming on pilgrimage to Jerusalem. The people of Jerusalem had recently known the shame and sorrow of exile, when they were carried from their homeland to a foreign nation. There, by the waters of Babylon, they had sat and wept. Having gone out full of tears, they had recently come home full of song. Now the prophet assures them that the very nations among whom they had been exiled will come on pilgrimage to Jerusalem. The pagan peoples will move out from under their darkness, drawn by the light of the Lord's glory that rises over Jerusalem. They are not really coming to the city but to the Lord; on their way they do not sing the praises of Jerusalem, but the praises of the Lord, because they recognise him as Saviour of all nations.

In today's gospel reading we have a smaller pilgrimage, but one of even greater significance. It is this little pilgrimage that brings us together in this church today. If the first reading speaks of nations and kings, the gospel reading speaks only of 'some wise men'. We are not told how many, although Christian iconography has always depicted three, on the basis of the three gifts. They come on pilgrimage to Judaea 'from the east'. Like all pilgrims, these wise men were seekers. They looked up beyond this earth towards the stars, far into deepest space. Looking up and out, they were led by one particular star to travel west in search of a new born Jewish child who had come, not just for the Jewish people, but for people like themselves, for all who were seekers after truth and light. As they drew near to their destination, they had a meeting with an earthly king who was the antithesis of God's infant king whom they were seeking. They brushed against evil in their search for the good; they looked into the face of violence and injustice on their way towards the king who would live and die in the cause of justice and peace. Yet, in spite of that dangerous moment, they reached their goal, and having found the child, they worshipped him. Their journey which began in hope ended in worship.

There are many gospel characters with whom we can find ourselves identifying. Different gospel characters express different dimensions of our human and Christian identity. The wise men from the east speak to the pilgrim within us. We are not always on holidays, but we are always on pilgrimage. We remain pilgrims until the end of our earthly life, in the words of Paul's letter to the Philippians, 'straining towards what lies ahead', and pressing 'on towards the goal'. The 'goal', 'what lies ahead', is not so much a place as a person, the person of Christ. Our ultimate destiny is to be 'conformed to the body of his glory'. Along the way, we too will have our brush with evil, but evil will not stop us in our tracks because, in the words of Paul's letter to the Romans, 'where sin increased, grace abounded all the more'. Our journey will end with worship, and every experience of worship on the way is an anticipation of our goal.

The Baptism of the Lord

With the Feast of the Baptism of the Lord, we know that we have left the liturgy of Christmas behind us. The child Jesus has now become an adult. It is as a full-grown man that he steps into the river Jordan to be baptised by John and to begin his public ministry. He leaves behind the sheltered life of Nazareth and he steps onto a more public stage. As he does so he experiences the coming of the Holy Spirit and he hears God say to him: 'You are my Son, the Beloved; my favour rests on you.' What a wonderful way to begin this significant new stage of his life – empowered by God's Spirit and assured of God's favour.

Unlike Jesus, most of us came to the waters of baptism as children, not as adults. We did not walk there as Jesus did; we were brought there by our parents. Our birth day is a day that gets remembered every year. There is something to be said for giving our baptism day a remembrance also. The early Christians paid at least as much attention to the day of Jesus' baptism as they did to the day of his birth. Indeed, the baptism of Jesus stood out more for the first Christians than his birth. They recognised that the day of Jesus' baptism was a kind of a watershed for him. This was the day when Jesus began to make an impact. Such was the impact Jesus made that it reverberated down the centuries, resulting in our presence here today in this church.

Indeed, it would not be an exaggeration to say that the day of our baptism was as significant a moment in our lives as the day of Jesus' baptism was in his life. Our baptism day was the day when God said to us what was said to Jesus on his baptism day: 'You are my son/my daughter, the beloved, my favour rests on you.' The same Holy Spirit who came down on Jesus on the day of his baptism came down on us on our baptism day. We started life blessed by God, graced by the Spirit of his love and by the word of his favour. We were of course too young to appreciate what was happening to us at the time. We were given a gift that would take a lifetime to unpack. That is why it is so important to revisit our baptism as adults, to journey back to that moment in our mind and heart, and in some way to experience it again.

Although the moment of baptism was shortly after birth for

most of us, the reality of baptism endures throughout our lives. The Spirit that God poured out upon us at baptism continues to work deep within us throughout our lives. The words of favour that God spoke to us back then, God continues to speak to us in the course of our lives. As adults, we have the opportunity to really receive that Spirit of God and to allow those words of favour to sink into us and to recreate us. Yet, it is because we are adults that we can find it so hard to receive his Spirit and to hear those words. We have lived enough of life to realise that we are not all we could be. As a result, we struggle to hear God say to us: 'My favour rests on you.' We could assume that those words are intended for others, not for me. Yet, God addresses those words to each of us personally.

It was in the power of the Holy Spirit and of God's word to him that Jesus began his public ministry. It is in the power of that same Spirit and that same word that each of us can set out on whatever journey the Lord is calling us to make at this time. In the first reading, God says to the prophet: 'I have made of you a witness to the people.' But before he spoke that word of mission to him, God said to him: 'Come to the water … pay attention, come to me.' The prophet is invited to receive before he is sent to minister. So it was for Jesus, and so it is for each of us. We need first to hear the call of God to come and drink, to drink of his Spirit and of his favour. Only then can we do what he is asking of us; only then can we really share in his Son's mission in the world. Today, the Feast of the Baptism of the Lord, we pray that each of us would experience anew the grace of our baptism, and commit ourselves afresh to living our baptismal calling to the full.

First Sunday of Lent

We are very aware at this time of the year that the days are beginning to get longer. The beginning of the season of Lent in the church's year always coincides with the beginning of spring in the seasonal year. Indeed, the word 'Lent' comes from the old English word for 'springtime'.

Just as spring is a time of new beginning in nature, so Lent is a season of new beginning in our own lives. The call of Lent is a call to personal renewal. This is the call of Jesus in today's gospel reading: 'Repent and believe the good news.' According to Mark's gospel this morning, Jesus' call to renewal was the second part of his opening message. The first part was, in a sense, more important: 'The time has come, and the kingdom of God is close at hand.' This is the heart of Jesus' good news. God's reign, God's rule, was close at hand. Jesus announced that God was powerfully present in a life-giving way through himself. This remains Jesus' message to us today. The call to renewal is a call to open our lives more fully to God who is powerfully present through his risen Son. The call of Lent is the call to turn towards God who comes towards us in Christ. This call will often entail turning away from whatever it is that might be preventing us from opening our lives more fully to God's presence. This turning away is what we mean by repentance. It will mean something different for each of us. In turning more fully towards God and away from what comes between God and ourselves, we will experience a new springtime of the Spirit.

Real renewal of this kind does not happen in an instant. It takes time, indeed, a lifetime. Lent is a season that gives us time. It is a long season in the church's year, seven weeks in all. We are given this time to help us to look at ourselves and to see what areas of our lives need renewal. This looking at ourselves is not meant to be a kind of navel gazing. We look at ourselves in the light of God's presence, in the light of the gospel. We first hear the good news as addressed to us personally, 'The kingdom of God is at hand', and in the light and joy of that good news we look at our lives. We try to discern whether our lives display God's kingdom, God's rule, whether they are governed by the values and attitudes of God as revealed to us by Jesus, as lived by him.

In that sense, Lent is a season when we try to take stock of ourselves. It is a time when the whole church is asked to go on a kind of retreat. When we think of a retreat, we tend to think of going away from the normal routine of life to a special place where there is a different routine. In the gospel reading we find Jesus doing just that. He is driven by the Spirit into the wilderness. He remains there for forty days, which is the length of our Lenten season. For us, however, Lent is not a retreat in that sense. The arrival of Lent does not mean that the rhythm of our lives changes in any fundamental way. We cannot head out into the wilderness. We have to live Lent in the midst of life. Our Lenten retreat does not mean a retreat from life in the literal sense. What it does mean is that we try to become more self-reflective. Because we are asked to reflect on ourselves, in the light of the gospel, it might to better to say that Lent is a time when we are called to become more prayerful. In prayer, we invite the Lord to show us those areas of our lives that are not in keeping with the call of the gospel and we ask the Lord to help us to change for the better where that is needed.

When Jesus went into the wilderness he was tested by Satan. He came face to face with the power that is opposed to the gospel. Jesus did not live the gospel without a struggle. If Jesus had to face the power that is opposed to the gospel, the same is true of his followers. There are forces outside of us and deep within us that are hostile to the values of the gospel. The first step in overcoming them is to face them as Jesus did. Lent is the time to do that. We do not do this on our own. We face them with the Lord, convinced that, as St Paul reminds us, where sin abounds, God's grace abounds all the more.

Second Sunday of Lent

Most of us would be aware of times in our lives when we did not do ourselves justice. The way we spoke or acted, the way we related to someone, did not really express our better self. We can show different faces to others, not all of them faces we would be proud of. Yet, even when we fall short of our better self, we know that we can set out again and make a new effort to let our best self shine through, the self that is made in the image and likeness of God.

We would all like people to judge us not on the basis of our off days but on the basis of our good days, the days that do us justice. You may have had the experience of forming a judgement of someone on the basis of some negative experience you had of them. Subsequently, you had a very different experience of them, you saw a different face of them, and you found that you had to revise your opinion of them for the better. We need to be open to seeing people with new eyes.

Unlike ourselves, Jesus did not show different faces to people. He always showed the same face, the face of God, because he was God in human form. He had no bad days, in that sense. Yet, many people perceived Jesus in ways that did not do him justice. Some of his opponents saw him in such a negative light that they considered him to be in league with Satan. Even Jesus' own followers had difficulty in seeing Jesus as he really was. At Caesarea Philippi, when Jesus declared himself to be the Son of Man who would suffer and die, Peter took him aside and began to rebuke him. One of the faces of God that Jesus showed was the face of a suffering God. This was a face that Peter and the other disciples were very uncomfortable with.

According to Mark's gospel, it was immediately after this clash between Jesus and his disciples at Caesarea Philippi that Jesus took them up the mount of the transfiguration. There, Jesus revealed another face of God, the glorious face of God, and Jesus himself was declared to be the Son of God. His disciples saw Jesus in a way they had never seen him before. They saw him with new eyes. The glorious face of God was a face that Peter was very much at home with. Indeed, Peter wanted to prolong this moment: 'It is wonderful for us to be here', he exclaimed, 'let us make three tents, one for you, one for Moses and one for Elijah.' However, Peter had to learn that the glorious Son of God who so enthralled him was also the suffering Son of Man who so repelled him. That is the significance of the word from the mountain addressed to Peter and the other disciples, 'Listen to him', listen to Jesus when he speaks of himself as the Son of Man who has to suffer and die. The two faces of God that Jesus displays, the suffering face and the glorious face, have to be held together.

Fundamentally, Jesus only reveals one face of God, the face of love. God's love for us, God's loyalty to us, was such that God was prepared to allow his Son to die for our sakes. Paul declares in today's second reading: 'God did not spare his own Son, but gave him up to benefit us all.' In today's first reading, Abraham's loyalty to God was so great that he was prepared to sacrifice his son to God. Abraham's loyalty to God is a sign of God's loyalty to us. God is so loyal to us that God is prepared to give us his Son, even though that entailed his cruel and untimely death. Jesus declared that no one has greater love than to lay down one's life for one's friends. Jesus' death on the cross revealed the face of God to be the face of a greater love. Here indeed is a love that is beyond any human love, a love that prompts Paul to ask his triumphant question at the beginning of today's second reading: 'With God on our side, who can be against us?'

Our calling as people who have been so loved by God in this way is to show the face of Christ, the face of God, to others. It is that face alone that will do us justice as people who have been baptised into the body of Christ and who have received the Spirit of Christ. Our ultimate destiny in heaven is to be conformed to the image of God's Son. Our calling is to show forth something of that image here and now.

Third Sunday of Lent

We all admire individuals or groups who see something wrong and commit themselves to putting it right. In our own country various groups over the years have formed around many issues because they feel some injustice has been done. Their passion for truth and justice gives them energy, even in the face of official indifference and stone-walling. It is often because they themselves have been personally affected by the issue in question that they keep pursuing it until they get an outcome that begins to put things right. We need such individuals and groups to keep us on our toes. It can take the passionate commitment of a few to bring home to us that there are serious matters here that need to be addressed.

Most of the Jews who used the Jewish temple in Jesus' day probably did not see any great problem with it. They had grown used to the ways things were done in the Temple precincts. However, when Jesus went into the Temple he saw it with very different eyes. His deep relationship with God as his Father alerted him to all that was wrong in the Temple: his Father's house had become a market. What should have been a place of worship had become a place of commerce. Jesus saw immediately that God's purposes were not being served by what was going on in the Temple. In a daring symbolic action Jesus expressed God's displeasure at what the Temple had become. He went further and declared that the Temple of stone would be replaced by a new temple, the temple of his risen body. This new temple would become the focus of a new kind of worship – worship in Spirit and in truth, as he said to the Samaritan woman. Because Jesus is the truth, worship in truth is a sharing in the risen Jesus' own worship of God, and this is made possible by the presence of the Holy Spirit in our lives. The Spirit who inspires us to cry out Abba, Father, as Jesus does, also works to bear rich fruit in our day to day lives, what Paul calls the fruit of love, joy, patience, kindness, faithfulness, gentleness, self-control. We could add also the fruit of a passion for justice and truth. Worship and daily living would be of a piece, inspired by the one Spirit of God.

In the gospel reading, Jesus showed himself to be a disturber of the peace, because the peace he found in the temple was not the peace of God. The risen Jesus continues to be a disturber of false peace today. He continues to challenge ways of relating between people that are not an expression of God's purpose. He continues to set himself against forms of worship that do not take God seriously. The disruptive Jesus that the gospel reading puts before us has not gone away. If we are really open to the risen Lord's presence in our lives we will come to share his sense of disturbance at all that is contrary to God's intention, whether that be in the church or in society. Taking on the task of disturbing people and situations that need disturbing will often cost us something. When the disciples saw Jesus acting against the practices of the Temple, they remembered the words of scripture, 'Zeal for your house will devour me.' Jesus' zeal to put right what was wrong literally devoured him; it put him on a cross. Taking a stand for the values of God, the values that are expressed in the Ten Commandments in today's first reading, will often carry a certain risk. Yet, this is the risk that the risen Lord often asks us to take. The risen Jesus does not ask us to stand alone. We take our stand with other believers in the Lord. We witness together to the values of the Father, revealed in the life, death and resurrection of his Son.

The stand that Jesus took in the Temple could be considered foolish. He was setting himself against powerful interest groups, which could only spell danger for him. Yet, as Paul states in today's second reading: 'God's foolishness is wiser than human wisdom.' Sometimes God may ask us to take a step that, from a merely human point of view, looks foolish and, yet, in reality is an expression of the wisdom and power of God.

Jesus took his stand in the Temple as God in human form. He could speak authoritatively of his Father's house. When we take a stand against something, we are aware that all is probably not right in our own lives. This awareness will keep us humble as we strive to give expression in our lives to the Lord's passion for the values of God's kingdom.

Light V Dark

Fourth Sunday of Lent

Children are often afraid of the dark, as the parents here in the church will know. A dim light is sometimes left on while children sleep, so that if they wake up it is not in pitch darkness. Many of us as adults find total darkness disconcerting too. Those of us who live in cities never really experience total darkness. The street lights dispel the darkness to some extent. It is different out in the country away from villages, towns and cities.

Although most of us would claim to prefer light to darkness, in today's gospel reading Jesus declares that some people 'have shown they prefer darkness to the light because their deeds were evil'. Most crime is committed during the hours of darkness. Those who are intent on doing wrong are drawn to darkness because it provides them with cover. As today's gospel states: 'Everyone who does wrong hates the light and avoids it, for fear his actions should be exposed.' One of the many security measures that have become popular in recent years is an array of bright lights that come on at night whenever anyone steps into an area that is out of bounds. Light is considered, with good reason, to be a deterrent to the person who is intent on committing crime. Indeed, there is a sense in which we all fear too much light just as we do too much darkness. Many of us prefer to stay in the background, in the shadows, and don't like the spotlight being shone on us. There are aspects of our lives that we would prefer to remain in darkness because we are not sure how people might respond to us if a bright light were to be shone on them. We only bring our deepest selves out into the light in the presence of those we really trust.

The gospel of John frequently refers to Jesus as light. In today's gospel reading, Jesus says with reference to himself: 'Light has come into the world.' The response of some to God's light coming into the world in the person of Jesus was to turn away from Jesus, to reject him. Indeed, some went so far as to try and extinguish the light, by lifting him up onto a cross. We resist bright lights if we think the light is going to be harsh and judgemental. However, today's gospel declares that the light that has come into the world in the person of Jesus is the light of God's love. In one of the most memorable statements of the New

Testament, the gospel reading declares: 'God loved the world so much that he gave his only Son so that everyone who believes in him ... may have eternal life.' The light of Jesus is not the probing light of the grand inquisitor that seeks out failure and transgression with a view to condemnation. Indeed, the gospel reading states that God 'sent his Son into the world not to condemn the world'. The light of Jesus, rather, is the inviting light of God's love.

At the beginning of today's gospel reading, Jesus speaks of himself as the Son of Man who must be lifted up. It was above all when Jesus was lifted up on the cross that the light of God's love shone most brightly. It is a paradox that those who attempted to extinguish God's light shining in Jesus only succeeded in making that light of love shine all the more brightly. God's gift of his Son to us was not in any way thwarted by the violent rejection of his Son. God's giving continued as Jesus was lifted up to die, and God's giving found further expression when God raised his Son from the dead and gave him to us as risen Lord. Here indeed is a light that darkness cannot overcome, a love that human sin cannot extinguish.

When we are going through a difficult experience and darkness seems to envelope us, it can be tempting to think that we will never see the light again. This is the mood that is captured in today's responsorial psalm: 'By the rivers of Babylon, there we sat and wept.' In such dark moments it is worth turning to that verse in the opening chapter of John's gospel: 'A light shines in the darkness and the darkness did not overcome it.' Here is a light that heals and restores. In the words of today's second reading, it brings us to life with Christ and raises us up with him. It shines in a special way whenever we celebrate the Eucharist. It is above all at the Eucharist that the light of God's love, revealed in the death and resurrection of Jesus, shines upon whatever darkness we may be struggling with in our lives.

Fifth Sunday of Lent

We can find ourselves faced with the prospect of doing something which we know is worth doing but which we also know is going to make demands on us. Faced with that kind of a situation we can experience something of a struggle within us. In our heart of hearts we want to do this worthwhile task and, yet, at another level we do not want to do it. Invariably, if we overcome our resistance and follow through on our good intention, we will feel afterwards that we did the right thing. It is probably true to say that we experience that kind of a struggle several times a week. As well as those daily struggles that are part of life, we may find ourselves engaged in a more fundamental struggle, where the future direction of our lives is at stake. I am thinking of those moments in our lives when we have a really important decision to make, and how we make it has enormous consequences for ourselves and for others. The right decision can often be the more difficult one, and the struggle in making it can be great indeed.

In today's gospel reading we find Jesus in just such a significant moment of decision. The hour when he has to leave this world is drawing near. The journey from this world to the Father will be painful and traumatic. As he faces into this hour, he asks aloud the question: 'What shall I say?' There are two possible answers to that question. He could ask the Father to preserve him from the hour and all that it entails: 'Father, save me from this hour.' Alternatively, he could ask the Father to be present to him as he heads into his hour. This in fact is the prayer he makes at this crucial moment in his life: 'Father, glorify your name.' Rather than the focus of his prayer being on himself, 'save me', the focus of his prayer is on God, 'glorify your name'. Rather than putting what he wants at the centre of his prayer, he puts what God wants to the fore. With the prayer, 'Father, glorify your name', Jesus commits himself anew to doing the work that the Father has given him, with all its consequences.

That question of Jesus, 'What shall I say?' or some version of it, can be a question that we find ourselves asking too. 'What shall I do? What path will I take?' Jesus took the path that God wanted him to take. That path involved a dying but it was a path that was ultimately life-giving, not only for himself but for a humanity. In our own lives, taking the path that God would want us to take will often involve some kind of dying for us, such as dying to our own comfort and convenience, letting go of the plans that we have for ourselves. This can take very ordinary forms. We get a phone call from someone who needs to talk to us, just as we are about to sit down and watch our favourite television programme. Someone asks us to visit them, and the only opportunity we have for doing that is Saturday afternoon when we would normally take it easy. A call for help goes out in regard to some issue and we know that we have the time and the ability to respond, but we also know that if we do so it will make demands on us. The strong temptation is to pray, 'Father, save me from this hour', to try and preserve ourselves, to protect ourselves. Yet, today's gospel makes a strong declaration that if we invest energy in trying to preserve ourselves, we will loose ourselves. 'Anyone who loves his life looses it.' If, on the contrary, we give ourselves away, we will find life. It is the grain of wheat that falls to the earth and dies that bears much fruit.

We are only a week away from Holy Week. During Holy Week we remember Jesus' readiness to fall to the ground and die for our sakes. As we contemplate his dying for us, we may find ourselves drawn to him. Jesus says in today's gospel reading: 'When I am lifted up from the earth, I will draw all people to myself.' It is in allowing ourselves to be drawn to him that we will find the strength to take the path that he took, the path of self-giving that leads to fullness of life. It is only our union with Christ which will empower us to take this path. Every day we invite the Lord to draw us to himself, so that we too can become the grain that falls to the ground and dies, and in dying bears much fruit.

Palm Sunday

ink of the journey of our lives in terms of colour
...e would probably find that we would need many different
colours to depict that journey. We might use the colour red to
depict those times when we gave of ourselves in love to serve
others in some generous way. This could be termed our last supper moments, remembering that it was at the last supper that
Jesus washed the feet of his disciples. We might use the colour
green to depict those experiences of newness and freshness,
those times when we began some new project with enthusiasm
and dynamism. These might be described as our Easter moments.

Undoubtedly, we would also find ourselves reaching for the
darker colours on our pallet from time to time. We might even
find it necessary to dip our brush into the black paint occasionally.
We would need that colour to depict those dark experiences that
are an inevitable part of all our lives. These will be the times
when we suffered in some deep way. The suffering may have
been physical or emotional or spiritual, or a combination of all
three. We might think of those times when we felt extremely
lonely, or when we had to endure some major disappointment,
or when we were unfairly treated or unjustly deprived of our
good name, when something was done to us by another that left
us feeling diminished. We might also think of times of great loss,
when we had to let go of someone whom we loved deeply. The
greatest loss of all is when our loved ones go on that final journey from this life to the next. When we look back on all these
moments in our lives, we remember them as traumatic, as
deeply painful and very draining. These might be termed our
Good Friday moments.

We have just read Mark's account of Jesus' Good Friday
moment. Each of the four evangelists tells this story, but Mark's
account is the darkest of all four. The account of John, which we
read every Good Friday, has the most light in it, and in between
Mark and John stand the accounts of Matthew and Luke, with
Matthew a little less dark than Mark and Luke a little less dark
again than Matthew. Mark depicts this experience of Jesus in
very dark colours indeed. The three disciples who were closest

to Jesus fall asleep in the garden; he is betrayed by Judas, one of the twelve, denied by Peter, the leader of the twelve, deserted by all his disciples at the moment of his arrest, falsely accused before the Jewish Sanhedrin, handed over to be crucified by a governor who surrendered his authority to the mob, jeered and mobbed as he hung dying on a cross, and with his last words crying out to God in deep desolation. From the moment Jesus shares his last supper with his disciples until the moment of his death, the story as Mark tells it seems to have no redeeming features. Apart from Jesus, everyone in the story is deeply flawed. Jesus goes to his death surrounded by the worst instincts of human nature.

Yet, in the midst of all this terrible darkness, the evangelist knows that there is a light for those with eyes to see it, the light of God's love and of God's presence. In the story as Mark tells it, a pagan recognises this light at the very moment when Jesus dies. The Roman centurion declares: 'Truly, this man was the Son of God.' He recognised the light of God's presence at the heart of all this darkness. This pagan had eyes to see the deeper meaning of these ugly and painful events. God was indeed working powerfully through the awfulness of Golgotha, bringing good out of evil, new life out of death, transforming a story of human sin and pain into a story of redemption.

The evangelist is saying to all his readers, to us, that God is at the heart of all our own darknesses. God is present in all of our Good Fridays, working in the same life-giving way as he did on that first Good Friday. God is not absent from our darkest moments, even when we find ourselves crying out: 'My God, my God, why have your forsaken me?' Even though there may be darkness over the whole land, over our own personal world, the light of God's life-giving presence continues to shine. We might pray on this Palm Sunday for the eyes of the centurion so that we too may recognise and worship the Lord present with us even in our darkest moments. 'Even though I walk through the valley of darkness, you are there with your crook and your staff. With these, you give me comfort.'

Holy Thursday

St Paul, in this evening's second reading, speaks of the night that Jesus was betrayed, the night before Jesus was crucified. It is that night that we celebrate this Holy Thursday evening. To speak of the night that Jesus was betrayed is to highlight the dark side of that particular night. Yet, the focus of our celebration this evening is on another, more positive, side of that night. It is on what Jesus did for us.

On the night he was betrayed, Jesus gave us the gift of the Eucharist. He gave himself to his disciples, and to all of us, under the form of bread and wine. As he would give himself to us on the cross the following afternoon, he anticipated that gift of himself to us that particular night. He then asked his disciples to repeat what he did in his name: 'Do this in memory of me', so that believers of every generation would personally experience the gift of himself that Jesus made on the night he was betrayed. On the very night when Jesus was handed over to his enemies by one of his own, Jesus handed himself over to his own. Every time we celebrate the Eucharist, the same Jesus, now risen Lord, hands himself over to us. Our very familiarity with the Eucharist can dull our appreciation of it. Holy Thursday is our annual opportunity to appreciate the extraordinary gift that the Eucharist is. The Word, who was with God in the beginning, now hands himself over to us under the form of bread and wine. It is no wonder we say together, by way of preparation to receive this tremendous gift: 'Lord, I am not worthy to receive you.' Perhaps at some deep level we realise that it is we who should be handing ourselves over to the Lord rather than he handing himself over to us.

It is that kind of sentiment that seems to be at work in Peter in today's gospel reading. Jesus got up from table, wrapped a towel around his waste, poured water into a basin and began to wash the feet of his disciples. Once again, Jesus was handing himself over to his disciples in a way that anticipated his handing over of himself to them and to all of us the following day on the cross. Jesus was pouring himself out in humble service of his disciples, just as he would soon pour out his life for them and for all. Peter strongly objected to this action of Jesus: 'You shall never wash my feet.' It was he who should be washing Jesus' feet and not the other way around. Yet, Jesus was insistent: 'If I do not wash you, you can have nothing in common with me.' This is the way Jesus does things; there is nothing to negotiate here. Both the institution of the Eucharist and the washing of the feet proclaim the presence of someone who came not to be served but to serve and to give his life as a ransom for all.

Peter had to learn to receive Jesus' love on Jesus' own terms, and we have to do the same. Jesus empties himself for us, as St Paul says: 'He emptied himself taking the form of a servant.' It is that self-emptying love of Jesus that was present at the washing of the feet and is present at every Eucharist. If we are not prepared to receive that love, unworthy as we may consider ourselves to be, Jesus will say to us what he said to Peter that evening: 'You can have nothing in common with me.' If we receive that extraordinary gift of self-emptying love, then we will hear the call that Peter and the other disciples heard on that first Holy Thursday: 'If I, the Lord and Master, have washed your feet, you should wash each other's feet', or as Jesus went on to say: 'Just as I have loved you, you also should love one another.' On that first Holy Thursday, Peter and the other disciples were greatly graced and greatly called. Every time we celebrate the Eucharist we are greatly graced and greatly called. That is why it is not something we do lightly. We are sent out from the Eucharist to serve others as we have been served by the Lord.

Tonight we celebrate the many servants among us, those who kneel at the feet of their brothers and sisters with no thought for recognition. We think of parents who serve their children, children who serve their parents, grandparents who serve their grandchildren and all who serve within the context of family life. Such servants are also present in our communities, in our parishes, in our neighbourhoods. Tonight's feast salutes them and assures them that they have much in common with the Word who became flesh and dwelt among us.

Good Friday

Many people find it easier to identify with the message of Good Friday that with the message of Easter Sunday. Perhaps that is because we are all familiar with the way of the cross in some shape or form, whereas the resurrection remains to a great extent a future hope. Yet, were it not for Easter Sunday, the Friday on which Jesus died would not have come to be known as 'Good' Friday. It is Easter that reveals the deeper meaning of the horrors of Golgotha. It is the light of Easter Sunday that makes sense of the darkness of Calvary. More that any of the other evangelists, John the evangelist has allowed the light of Easter to shine upon the events of Jesus' passion and death. We have just heard his telling of the story of those events.

The last words of Jesus in John's account are, 'I am thirsty', and 'It is accomplished.' The evangelist was very aware that Jesus' words, 'I am thirsty' expressed more that just the physical thirst of a dying man. When a thirsty Jesus met a Samaritan woman at a well, he said to her: 'Give me a drink.' Yet, Jesus' physical thirst for water on that occasion revealed a deeper thirst, and that was his thirst, his desire, to offer this woman, and her people, living water, the living water of the Spirit, the living water of God's love. That is why he 'had to go through Samaria' (Jn 4:4). Jesus promised the Samaritan woman that this living water of the Spirit would become in her a bubbling spring that would well up to eternal life and that would enable her to worship in Spirit and in truth.

Jesus' cry from the cross, 'I thirst', expresses this deeper thirst in his life to pour out the living water of God's life, of God's love, on all who look upon him with the eyes of faith. For the fourth evangelist, this is the meaning of the flow of blood and water that came from the side of Jesus after he was pierced. The life-giving water of the Spirit of God's love pours out from Jesus upon all who gather at the foot of the cross in faith, upon the mother of Jesus, the beloved disciple, Nicodemus, Joseph of Arimathea, upon all of us who approach the crucified and risen Lord with open hearts. Earlier in John's gospel, Jesus had issued an invitation to one and all, an invitation he continues to issue to all of us gathered here on this Good Friday: 'Let anyone who is thirsty come to me, and let the one who believes in me drink. As the scripture has said, "Out of his heart shall flow rivers of living water".' We gather here this afternoon to drink again from those rivers of living water that flow from the heart of Jesus. We gather, conscious of that deep thirst in our own lives for a love that accepts us as we are, that forgives all that needs forgiving in us, that recreates and renews us, that empowers us to live as God meant us to live, to worship as God wants us to worship, a worship in Spirit and truth.

Our second reading this afternoon calls on us to be confident in approaching the throne of grace. In John's gospel the cross of Jesus becomes a royal throne, a throne of God's grace. Jesus is lifted up in all his royal splendour, and from the throne of the cross he pours out upon all God's scattered children the abundant waters of God's grace and love. As we approach to venerate the cross in a few moments, we remind ourselves that we are approaching the throne of God's grace and, in doing so, we are assured, in the words of that second reading, that we 'shall have mercy from him and find grace when we are in need of help'.

Having approached the throne of grace, and having drunk deeply from the wells of salvation, we are called to become beloved disciples. That is the call of Good Friday. Like the beloved disciple at the foot of the cross, we are invited to look to Mary as our mother, to Jesus as our brother, and to God as our Father. Like that beloved disciple, we are called to open our hearts to the love of Jesus and to love Jesus and one another as he has loved us. Like him, we are called to recognise the Lord's presence on the shore of our lives. Like him, we are sent forth to testify, to witness to the Lord before others. We pray for a few moments in silence that we would be receptive to the grace and also faithful to the call of Good Friday.

Easter Vigil

I am sure many of us will have had to make a sad walk in our time. It might have been a walk to the bedside of someone close to us who was very ill, or a walk to some neighbour to sympathise at a time of bereavement, or even a walk to the grave of a close relative or friend. These kinds of walks take their toll on us; they can leave us drained of life and energy. Tonight's gospel reading begins with such a walk. Mary of Magdala and the other women walk to the tomb of Jesus. They had walked with him around Galilee and then they had walked with him from Galilee to Jerusalem. They had looked on from a distance as Jesus hung dying from the cross; they had seen Joseph of Arimathea place the body of Jesus in his own new tomb and roll a great stone over the door of the tomb. Now they walked towards the tomb. Even in death, they could not separate themselves from the person who had given meaning and purpose to their lives.

Following their sad walk towards the tomb, the women heard good news from a young man in a white robe who was seated in the tomb: 'You are looking for Jesus of Nazareth, who was crucified: he has risen, he is not here.' That is the same good news that brought us to the church here tonight: 'Jesus is not dead; he is risen; he is alive and living among us.' The Lord has risen for all his followers, not just for the women. The women were also told that the risen Lord 'is going before you to Galilee; it is there you will see him'. The same risen Lord goes before all of us. We do not have to go to Galilee to meet the risen Lord. We can meet him wherever we happen to be. This is the good news that we celebrate this Easter night.

The women in tonight's gospel reading journeyed from the sadness of Good Friday to the joy of Easter Sunday. The journey they travelled on that first Easter Sunday was geographically short, but it was spiritually immense. Their journey was the Easter journey; it is a journey we can all travel with them. Our short journey into the church tonight behind the Paschal candle is a powerful symbol of what our whole lives as Christians are about. We are followers of a risen Lord. As the risen Lord went ahead of his first followers into Galilee, so he is always going ahead of us. The Lord desires to journey with us, to meet with us. What he wants from us is a corresponding desire to journey with him, to meet with him, the same desire that drove the women to go to the tomb on that first Easter Sunday, the desire that led the two disciples on the road to Emmaus to say to the stranger: 'Stay with us; it is towards evening.' Easter is the time to renew our desire to meet the Lord who desires to meet us.

When the risen Lord met the disciples after he rose from the dead, he met them in their brokenness. They were full of sadness at their loss, full of remorse at their own failure, full of confusion over how everything had turned out. They were a spent force. Yet, the Lord met them where they were. That is how we will often be when the Lord meets us. We search for him out of our pain and loss and, perhaps, remorse. Because the Lord is risen, our search will never be in vain. When he comes to us, he will call us to look beyond what is troubling us and to look towards him. He will call on us to look towards him in prayer, to worship him as we are doing tonight, and in our worship of him to find joy in our sadness, strength in our weakness, and peace in our remorse. When we look towards him in worship we will also hear him calling us to go forth as his messengers, to set out on his mission, as the women were sent out in tonight's gospel reading. He will send us out to bring the good news of his risen presence to all who need to hear it. 'Go', he will say to us, 'tell his disciples ... you will see him.' We are sent out to help others to see the face of the risen Lord that we have seen. Even more than that, we are sent out to show the face of the risen Lord to others through the quality of our presence to them. We pray this Easter night for the grace to be faithful to that wonderful calling.

Easter Sunday

Many of us would say that the people who know us best are those who love us most. Those who have given themselves in love to each other over many years know each other in a way that no one else knows them. Those we claim to know we often do not really know because we have no real connection with them.

In John's gospel one of Jesus' disciples is always referred to as the disciple that Jesus loved. The fourth evangelist believed that there was a very special bond between Jesus and this disciple. Here was a disciple who was completely open to the presence of God's love in the person of Jesus and who responded fully to that love. For the fourth evangelist, this disciple is the ideal disciple, the disciple we are all called to become. He is portrayed in the fourth gospel as someone who, because of his special bond of love with Jesus, knew Jesus better than any of the other disciples. Here was someone whose knowledge of Jesus was born of a greater love. He saw more clearly and more deeply than others. In this morning's gospel reading, he alone saw the true significance of the empty tomb of Jesus. In the words of the gospel reading: 'He saw and believed.' On the basis of the empty tomb alone, he recognised that Jesus had been raised from the dead. The other disciples came to this realisation only after the risen Lord appeared to them.

What the beloved disciple recognised, what he believed, is what brings us together here on this Easter Sunday: God has raised his Son to new life. This is the heart of our Christian faith. As St Paul says in his first letter to the Corinthians: 'If Christ has not been raised, then our proclamation has been in vain and your faith has been in vain.' If Jesus had not been raised from the dead, his life and work would have been a glorious, but nonetheless tragic, failure. Without Jesus' resurrection from the dead, what he began would have petered out. The resurrection was God's resounding 'yes' to all that Jesus said and did, to all that he lived and died for. In raising his Son from the dead, God raised up all that Jesus proclaimed by his words and deeds, by his life and death. Because of Jesus' resurrection, we can recognise his life and death as the manifestation of God's love and the revelation of God's will for our lives. That is why Easter, and not Christmas, is the most important feast in the church's year. That is why the season of Easter is seven weeks long, running right up to the feast of Pentecost.

We celebrate this great feast of Easter with flowers and song and alleluias, not only because it has to do with Jesus, but because it has to do with all of us. Christ's triumph over death is also our triumph. Through baptism we all share in Christ's triumph, we have been plunged into Christ's risen life. As Paul says in his letter to the Romans: 'The Spirit of him who raised Jesus from the dead dwells in you.' The Spirit is the first fruit of that fullness of life that Jesus now lives and that we are all destined to inherit. Because Jesus has been raised from the dead, all of us who have been baptised into him and are united with him through faith are Easter people. We live in the light of Easter.

If you were to find an image of the Christian life in today's gospel reading, it would not be the sad journey of Mary Magdalene to the tomb in the darkness; it would be much more the excited running to the tomb of the beloved disciple and Peter in the early light or, even more so, the subsequent journey of Mary Magdalene who, having met the risen Lord, went to the disciples to announce: 'I have seen the Lord.' Because of Easter, because of our conviction that in the person of Christ life has triumphed over death, we can approach with expectation whatever it might be in our life that seems to be a tomb, trusting that signs of new life are to be found there. Because of Easter we know that even our darkest moments, our Golgotha experiences, are bathed in the light of the risen Christ. Because of Easter we are also sent forth, like Mary Magdalene, as messengers of the risen Lord. Easter commits us to resisting all forms of death and violence; it commissions us to be channels of God's vibrant life to all who are in darkness and the shadow of death. In renewing our baptism this morning, we renew our response to that Easter commission.

Second Sunday of Easter

We know that fear can be very disabling. We often hold back from saying something because we are fearful of how it will be received. If we suspect that someone is going to oppose us for doing something, our tendency is not to proceed with it, even though we might know in our heart of hearts that it is worthwhile. Fear of others can hold us back and inhibit our growth as human beings.

This morning's gospel introduces us to a group of fearful disciples. It is the evening of the first day of the week, Easter Sunday, but the disciples are locked away in fear. The fear which caused them to abandon Jesus in his hour of need continues to take hold of them. They fear those who put Jesus to death, suspecting that what they did to Jesus they could do to them. It may be Easter Sunday, but the shadow of Golgotha hangs over them. The risen Lord comes to his fearful disciples. The evangelist simply states: 'He stood among them.' Standing is often a sign of strength and confidence. When we stand we assert that we are here. We speak of people standing on their own feet, or standing their ground. The Lord stood in all the strength of his risen life. This was a life that no one could take from him. In standing among them, the Lord led his disciples from fearfulness to boldness, from weakness to strength; he enabled them to leave their self-imposed prison and to go forth as his messengers of Easter good news. The gospel reading states that from being full of fear they were now filled with joy.

We may be able to identify rather easily with the group of fearful disciples in this morning's gospel reading. Fear of others can prevent us from witnessing to our faith. The culture in which we live encourages us to think of our faith as something very private, to be given expression to only behind the closed doors of our churches. There can be an intolerance of any public expression of faith. We may be committed to the values of the Lord's gospel, but we can be tempted to hide that commitment from others, fearing ridicule or rejection if we declare where we really stand. We need the risen Lord to stand among us as much as the first disciples did, and we can be assured that he does stand among us. He breathes the Holy Spirit on us as he did on those disciples. The seven week Easter season which we are beginning is the time to draw strength from the risen Lord who stands among us.

As well as being able to identify with the fearful disciples, we may also recognise something of ourselves in doubting Thomas. He had not been with the other disciples when the risen Lord appeared to them. He had moved away from the community of disciples. There may be times in our own lives when, like Thomas, we do not want the company of other disciples. We go apart from the church, the family of believers. There can be all kinds of reasons for this. When the disciples went looking for Thomas in their excitement and declared to him, 'We have seen the Lord', Thomas gave them short shrift – 'Unless I see … unless I put …' Thomas was not ready to return to the fold; he continued to keep his distance. He was an honest man; he was true to himself, even though that meant putting a distance between himself and the other disciples.

It seems that the Lord respected Thomas' honesty. When he appeared again to the disciples, this time with Thomas present, he accommodated himself to Thomas' request. There was no rebuke, only an invitation to believe. In response to the Lord's invitation, Thomas made one of the greatest confessions of faith in the gospels: 'My Lord and my God.' Those who have drifted from the community of believers often go on to become people of deep faith who show others the way. The story of Thomas shows us that scepticism and doubt are not necessarily the enemies of faith. It is in being true to ourselves – including our doubts – that we find the Lord or, rather, that the Lord finds us. Thomas did not travel to Easter faith at the same pace as the other disciples. No two journeys of faith are the same. The Lord is always ready to meet us where we are.

Thomas belatedly joined the group who saw and believed. We who gather here this morning belong to a different group. We are among those who have not seen and yet believe. In this morning's gospel reading the risen Lord declares us blessed. Here is a beatitude that embraces us all.

Third Sunday of Easter

Most of us, if we look back over our lives, will find something or other that we very much regret. We will almost certainly be able to identify times when we failed to live up to the values that we try to live by. Sometimes these experiences of personal failure can leave us very burdened. We can find it hard to move on from them; they trouble us and we struggle to be free of them. We can find ourselves going back in memory to them over and over again.

The first disciples of Jesus must have felt like this in the aftermath of Jesus' crucifixion. They had all deserted the one who had given them so much of himself. Their mood in the aftermath of Good Friday can only have been one of deep regret. They must have felt that their relationship with Jesus was over, and deservedly so. In this morning's gospel, however, the first words that the risen Jesus speaks to his disciples when he appears to them are 'Peace be with you.' These are words of reconciliation that sought to assure the disciples of the Lord's forgiveness. For those first disciples, the initial experience of the risen Lord took the form of a profound experience of forgiveness. The gift of forgiveness can be difficult to receive at times. We wonder if we are really forgiven. According to the gospel reading, when Jesus said, 'Peace be with you', the disciples responded with alarm and fright and thought that they might be seeing a ghost. It took the disciples a while to realise that they were forgiven.

It is only after the disciples had come to receive this gift of forgiveness that they could be sent out as messengers of the Lord's forgiveness to others. According to our gospel reading, the risen Lord, having assured them that they were forgiven, went on to commission them to preach repentance for the forgiveness of sins to all the nations. It is forgiven sinners who are entrusted with the task of proclaiming to all the good news of God's forgiving love. This is what we find Peter doing in today's first reading. He declares to the people of Jerusalem that, although they had handed Jesus over to Pilate, God's forgiveness was available to those who turn to God by believing in Jesus. In raising his Son from the dead, God was declaring that even when we reject God's Son, God does not reject us. The risen

Jesus reveals a faithful, forgiving God. Today's second reading states this clearly: 'If anyone does sin, we have our advocate with the Father, Jesus Christ, who is just.'

Before we can receive the Easter gift of God's forgiveness that comes to us through the risen Lord, we must first acknowledge our need of that gift. In the words of today's second reading, we need 'to admit the truth'. The truth is that we are always in need of the gift of God's forgiveness. Recognising our need and, in the light of that, asking God for that gift is what we call repentance. The risen Lord in the gospel reading sends out his disciples to preach repentance for the forgiveness of sins. Within the Catholic tradition, the Sacrament of Reconciliation is a privileged opportunity to admit the truth, to acknowledge our need of God's forgiveness and to ask for it. In that sacrament the risen Lord says to us, 'Peace be with you.'

The first disciples, having received the gift of the Lord's forgiveness, were sent out as heralds of that forgiveness to others. In a similar way, we who receive the same gift are sent out on the same mission. As forgiven sinners we proclaim with our lives the presence of a forgiving and faithful God. We extend to others the gift we have received from the Lord. This will not always come easy to us. It has been said that 'to err is human, to forgive is divine'. If that is true, we need divine help to do what is divine. In the verses that immediately follow where today's gospel ends, the risen Jesus promises his disciples that he would send the Holy Spirit upon them. It is only in the power of the Holy Spirit that they would be able to engage in the task that Jesus was entrusting to them. We need the same Spirit if we are to forgive as we have been forgiven. In the weeks ahead that precede the feast of Pentecost, we might pray the prayer: 'Come Holy Spirit, fill my heart and enkindle in me the fire of your love.' We could pray this prayer especially during those times when we find ourselves struggling to pass on to others the gift of forgiveness that we continue to receive from the Lord.

Fourth Sunday of Easter

When several people are interviewed for a job, the one person who comes through the interview process is not always the best candidate for the job. Interviewing is not an exact science. It can happen that one of those turned down for the job might have been the most suitable candidate. In the words of today's first reading, one of the rejected candidates may well have proven to be the corner stone had he or she been given the chance. Even the most qualified interview panel has only limited vision.

Sometimes what we think little of can turn out to be very valuable. I occasionally watch the *Antiques Roadshow* on BBC 1, and I am always amused when someone discovers that something or other that had been lying around in the attic for years is worth a fortune. The look of shock and amazement on people's faces is a sight to behold. In the 1940s a series of caves above the level of the Dead Sea, that no one had paid any attention to for hundreds of years, were discovered to contain jars of scrolls that went back to the time of Jesus and earlier. The discovery of these scrolls has had enormous implications for our understanding of the world into which Jesus was born. These very ordinary caves turned out to contain a very extraordinary treasure.

Real quality can be found in unpromising places. The gospels suggest that Jesus had that capacity to see quality where others saw nothing of consequence. In the gospel reading, Jesus, the good shepherd, says of himself: 'I know my own and my own know me.' He saw more deeply than other people saw. On one occasion, he saw a poor widow put two small copper coins into the temple treasury. Most people would hardly have noticed this woman. However, Jesus not only noticed her, but called over his disciples and drew their attention to her. Even though, in comparison to what the wealthy were giving, what she gave was tiny, Jesus singled her out as someone who, in reality, gave everything, all she had to live on. He saw her as a type of himself who would soon give all he had on the cross. She was an image of the good shepherd in today's gospel reading who lays down his life for the flock. Jesus pointed to her as the disciples' teacher. On an earlier occasion those same disciples had tried to block children from drawing near to Jesus. In the eyes of the disciples, they were clearly of no consequence. Jesus rebuked his disciples and insisted that the children be allowed to approach him. He then pointed to the children as the disciples' teachers, saying to them: 'Whoever does not receive the kingdom of God as a little child will never enter it.' Jesus knew that the stone that was prone to being rejected was often the key stone.

Today is Vocations Sunday. What is our vocation as people who have been baptised into Christ, who are members of Christ's body? One aspect of that vocation is learning to see as Jesus sees. We could say that a Christian is someone who sees life as Jesus does. What distinguished Jesus' way of seeing was its generosity. He saw more than others saw. Where others saw a stone to be rejected, he saw a corner stone. Where others saw children and widows as people of no significance, he saw them as people who had much to teach us. Whenever we see people with generous eyes and relate to them accordingly, we help them to become who they really are in God's eyes, like the cripple in today's first reading who, through Peter's presence to him, came to stand up perfectly healthy. The reverse is equally true. We can have a crippling effect on people when the stance we take towards them is critical and dismissive.

The way Jesus saw people was a reflection of how God sees us. In today's second reading, we read that God sees us as his children, as his sons and daughters: 'Think of the love that the Father has lavished on us by letting us be called God's children.' We are sons and daughters with a future, destined to see God as God really is. If we really saw others as sons and daughters of God, we would be slow to reject them, much less harm them, because we would realise that in rejecting them we were rejecting God. In the gospel reading, Jesus speaks of the hireling who abandons the sheep and runs away. To abandon others is to reject them. Vocations Sunday reminds us that we are called to be good shepherds in the way we relate to each other rather than hirelings, treasuring others rather than rejecting them.

Fifth Sunday of Easter

We live in an age that tends to put a high value on independence. We like to feel that we are free to make our own decisions. One of the aspects of reaching old age that can trouble many people is the prospect of loosing their independence. Most of us hate to think of ourselves becoming overly dependent on others. We want to be as independent as possible for as long as possible. Yet, we are also aware that independence is a relative thing. We know that, in reality, we depend on each other in all kinds of ways all the time. We are totally dependant on others at the beginning of life and, probably, for many of us, at the end of life as well. In between the beginning and end of life, we never escape fully from that dependency on others. In the living of our lives, there will always be a certain tension between the need to assert our independence of others and the need to acknowledge our dependence on others. Learning to negotiate well that tension is one of life's tasks.

The gospel's perspective on that basic tension in human life tends to put more emphasis on our dependence than on our independence. In this respect, as in other respects, the gospel message is at odds with the culture in which we live. The gospel strongly proclaims our ultimate dependence on God, and also our dependence on each other to the extent that one of the primary ways that God is present to us is through each other. The first Christians had a stronger sense than perhaps we do of their dependence on each other if they were to become all that God was calling them to be. St Paul's vision of the church as the body of Christ expresses the awareness that believers had of themselves as members of a community who were mutually interdependent. Paul himself, the great theologian, missionary and pastor was very aware of his dependence on others in the church. In today's first reading Luke describes a moment in Paul's early life as a Christian when he was very dependent on others. He had only recently changed from being the zealous opponent of the church to being one of its most enthusiastic supporters. He very much wanted to join the community of disciples in Jerusalem but, understandably, they were all afraid of him and kept him at a distance. It took a respected leader, Barnabas, to convince others that Paul could be trusted. Paul went on to be a much more significant person in the early church than Barnabas was and, yet, he was completely dependent on Barnabas to create that initial opening for him. Paul was aware that his dependence on Barnabas, and on others in the course of his life, was an expression of his dependence on the Lord.

The image of the vine in the gospel reading expresses the extent to which we as believers are dependant on other believers and, ultimately, on the Lord, if we are to live as the Lord's disciples. Jesus states: 'A branch cannot bear fruit all by itself.' We cannot live fruitful lives as Christians by going it alone. We need the community of believers if we are to become all that our baptism calls us to be. We need to be connected in some way into the community of faith, what we call the church. It is only in communion with other believers that our lives can bear the fruit of the Spirit. It is in and through other believers that the Lord can nurture our faith. That community of believers we need to be in communion with will often be a mixed bag. Yet, it is there that we find the Lord in a privileged way; it is through our connection with the church that we are connected to him. That connection with the Lord is vital because if we are to live our baptism to the full, it is on him that we are ultimately dependent. We need the Lord if our lives are to bear the fruit of the Spirit. As Jesus states in the gospel reading: 'Cut off from me you can do nothing.'

If we are dependent on the Lord, there is a sense in which he is also dependant on us. In the gospel reading Jesus says: 'Whoever remains in me bears fruit in plenty.' We would all consider fruit to be healthy food; it is an important source of nourishment. Lives that bear fruit in plenty are lives that nourish others, that are life-giving for others. The Lord depends on us to feed each other with his love and presence. If we are to do this, we need to be connected to him and to his followers.

Sixth Sunday of Easter

Some people have a lot of friends and others have a small circle of friends. We all need to befriend someone and to be befriended by someone; if that need is not met we are likely to feel that something important is missing from our lives. In a good and happy marriage the two spouses will be one another's best friends. This is a special kind of friendship, where two people share life in a very special way. For those who are not married or for married people who have become separated, for whatever reason, friendship will take a somewhat different form. It will not have that quality of intimacy that is found in a good marriage and, yet, the friendship can be very deep and lasting, and hugely significant for the two people involved. Many of us will have had friends in the past but, for whatever reason, we will have moved on from them and they will have moved on from us. However, we may also be able to point to people who have been our friends for many years and who are likely to remain life-long friends. We know that a life-long friendship does not happen automatically. Each of the two people in the friendship has to work at it.

In this morning's gospel reading, Jesus uses the language of friendship to describe his relationship with his disciples. He says: 'I shall not call you servants any more ... I call you friends.' He relates to us not as master to servant but as friend to friend. The relationship between a master and a servant is an unequal one. One aspect of this lack of equality is the absence of any mutuality. The master is likely to know the servant's business; he can walk into the servant's quarters when and as he likes. However, as Jesus remarks in the gospel reading: 'A servant does not know his master's business.' The world of the master is closed to the servant, but not vice-versa.

Jesus had already declared in John's gospel that as the good shepherd he knows his flock individually. The good shepherd 'calls his own by name and leads them out'. Because Jesus calls us friends and not servants he invites us to know him by name as he knows us by name. He has made it possible for us to know him intimately because he has revealed himself to us, as he says in this morning's gospel reading: 'I have made known to you everything I have learnt from my Father.' Jesus has spoken to us about the most intimate relationship in his life, his relationship with his Father. He has revealed his heart and his soul, his inner depths, to us, and the record of that self-revealing is to be found in the gospels. At the heart of a true friendship is the willingness to share deeply. In today's gospel reading, Jesus reminds us that he has shared deeply with us. He calls on us to share as deeply with him as he has shared with us. For us who are the Lord's disciples today, prayer is a moment when we can share our deepest selves with the Lord, opening our hearts to him as he has opened his heart to us. This sharing of our selves with the Lord is a form of prayer that is deeply rooted in the Jewish and Christian tradition. In prayer we are invited to be open and transparent before the Lord. We do not need to censure what we might share with the Lord; he will receive it all graciously as any true friend would.

If the readiness to share deeply is one sign of a true friendship, another sign is the readiness to put ourselves out for a friend in a way that may seem foolish to others. In our dealings with our closest friends we can find within ourselves a freedom to give generously that is not there when it comes to others. This is how Jesus has related to us. In today's gospel reading he states: 'A man can have no greater love than to lay down his life for his friends.' He speaks of his death on the cross as a profound act of befriending. He has not only shared deeply with us, but he has given fully of himself to us. He offers his friendship in this way not to a chosen few but to all who are open to receive it. As the first reading states: 'God does not have favourites.' Jesus calls on us to befriend one another as he has befriended us. This is a very challenging call. It may ask of us that we befriend people that we would not naturally befriend, that we reveal to others the God who does not have favourites.

The Ascension of the Lord

You often hear people say: 'I don't like goodbyes.' Many of us can easily identify with that sentiment. We know from our own experience that goodbyes can be painful. We may not like good-byes, but we cannot avoid them. The most traumatic goodbye is around the death of a loved one. We would do anything to avoid having to face into that particular goodbye. Yet, it is so often the case that we are helpless before what is happening, and we have to learn to face into the goodbye that we had hoped to put off. Most people somehow find it possible to let go, even though it can take time. Eventually they may go on to discover that letting go of someone in death does not mean the end of the relation-ship. They begin to relate to their loved one in a different way; they may come to understand the person in a way they had never done before.

The ascension of Jesus involved for his disciples some ele-ment of letting go of him. When Jesus was put to death on a cross, his disciples must have felt that they would never see him again. Then, to their amazement, he began to appear to them, and they realised that he had been raised from the dead. The time came when even those very reassuring appearances of the risen Lord came to an end, and he was no longer present to his followers in a visible form. We like people who are significant for us to be visible to us. Seeing the face of someone we love can mean more than all the phone calls and emails put together. That is why at the departure lounges of airports we keep our loved ones in view for as long as possible. We stare after our loved ones who are leaving us.

The first reading states that the disciples were staring into the sky. Yet, the question was immediately put to them: 'Why are you men from Galilee standing here looking into the sky?' Somehow, such looking skywards was not appropriate. It was not appropriate because in returning to the Father, the risen Lord had not really left them at all. Although no longer visible, he remained present to them. That is why today's feast is much more a celebration of the Lord's presence than a lament for the Lord's absence. Today's gospel reading expresses that very well. While stating that the Lord Jesus was taken up into heaven, it immediately declares that the Lord was working with the disciples as they proclaimed the gospel. He was taken from them and at the same time he was working *with* them. The emphasis of today's feast is on the second element, the Lord working *with* all of us.

We often use the phrase 'eternal rest' to refer to that life into which we pass beyond death. The New Testament strongly suggests that when Jesus returned to the Father, he did not enter into eternal rest. On the contrary, as risen Lord he was working with the disciples. He works with us today. God is at work through the risen Lord, as Jesus states in John's gospel: 'My Father is still working, and I also am working.' What is that work? The Lord's work today is in keeping with his work in Galilee, Judea and Samaria two thousand years ago. The Lord is at work bringing life where there is death, healing where there is brokenness, hope where there is despair. He is working to liberate people from all that diminishes and dehumanises them. He is working to reconcile those who are at enmity with each other. He is at work lifting people beyond the blindness and prejudice that leads to discrimination and much worse.

We need to remind ourselves today more than ever that the Lord is at work, that he returned to his Father precisely to do his work on a scale that was not possible when he walked the hills of Galilee and the streets of Jerusalem. The Lord looks to all of us to get involved in his work. The gospel reading presents the Lord working with his disciples; he needs disciples today to work with and through, as much as he did in the first century. According to our second reading today, the first thing the Lord did when he returned to his Father was to distribute gifts to his followers so that they could involve themselves in his work. We can be sure that he is not sparing with his gifts today. The Feast of the Ascension is a good opportunity for each of us to ask ourselves how the Lord might be gifting us, with a view to our sharing in his work.

Pentecost Sunday

As soon as we emerge into the light of day at birth we begin to communicate with those around us. The crying of the new born baby is an initial attempt to communicate. As new born babies begin to grow, their efforts to communicate become more articulate. They begin to speak their first words and before long they start to shape phrases and then to put sentences together. The ability to communicate in writing comes later, through their schooling. Children learn to communicate reasonably quickly. Before they have reached the age of twelve, most children will have acquired the basic communication skills of speaking and writing.

Yet, we know from our experience that the challenge to communicate well is a life-long one. As children move into the teenage years, they can struggle to communicate with others. As they become aware of depths within themselves, they often don't find it easy to communicate from out of those depths, even with those to whom they are closest. Children can have a wonderful openness and spontaneity, but they tend to loose that as they move into their teenage years. As teenagers move into their adult years, they can form deeper relationships with people and in that context a deeper form of communication becomes possible. Yet, we are all aware that we do not always communicate well as adults. What we think we are communicating and what people actually hear can be quite different. At another level still, we can communicate one thing but actually, in our heart of hearts, believe something else. When we say what we don't mean and don't say what we mean, the consequences are invariably chaotic. People don't know where they stand, and there is a breakdown in trust and cohesion.

When the Holy Spirit came upon the first disciples of Jesus on that first Pentecost, according to Luke, they received an ability to communicate in a way they had never communicated before. There were Jews present in Jerusalem from all over the Roman Empire of the time. They would have spoken a great variety of languages and yet, they were able to say: 'Each of us hears the disciples in our own native language.' The Spirit at work among the disciples broke down the language barriers that are normal obstacles to communication. The Spirit gave the disciples a new gift of speech; they were enabled to witness to the marvels of God in a way that people from other cultures and language groups could understand and receive. One of the signs that the Spirit is at work is when there is real communication between people about the marvels of God, when something of the good news of what God has done for us in Jesus is proclaimed in a way that is received by others.

The Spirit of God comes to help us to communicate with each other about the Lord, to build communion in the Lord. St Paul had this same understanding of the Holy Spirit. In today's second reading he states that 'What the Spirit brings is love, joy, peace, patience, kindness, goodness, trustfulness, gentleness and self-control.' These are qualities that we associate with the Lord. The Spirit comes to form these qualities within us so that by living these qualities we can communicate the Lord to each other and be in deeper communion with each other. Whenever we display any of those qualities, we are communicating the Lord to one another and the Spirit is at work among us. St Paul was convinced that we cannot communicate the Lord to each other without the help of the Holy Spirit. We need to pray, 'Come Holy Spirit, fill our hearts', if we are to communicate the Lord to each other.

We can only communicate the Lord to each other if we know the Lord ourselves. It is the Holy Spirit who helps us to know the Lord – and to know him not just with our heads but with our hearts. This is the message of St John in today's gospel reading. The role of the Holy Spirit is to lead us to the complete truth, to lead us to Jesus who *is* the Truth. We need the Holy Spirit if we are to come to know the Lord and, so, communicate the Lord to others in what we say and do. Because the Holy Spirit is so necessary to us in our Christian lives, the Lord is not slow to share the Spirit with us. Pentecost is not a once-off event. The Lord continues to pour out the Holy Spirit on all those who ask for this gift. On this Feast of Pentecost, we ask for a fresh outpouring of the Spirit on each of us, so that, like the first disciples, we will come to know the Lord and be able to communicate him to each other today.

Feast of the Most Holy Trinity

It is probably true to say that most of us know only a few people really well. A husband and wife may know more or less all that there is to know about each other; the same could be said of two people who have been very close friends for many years. Yet, even those who spend a lot of time in each other's company do not necessarily know each other deeply. Parents do not always know their children in this deep sense and *vice versa*. We are complex and mysterious beings, all of us. Not only are we complex but most of us do not find it easy to reveal ourselves to someone.

If we struggle to grasp each other, what chance do we have of grasping God? God is infinitely more mysterious than any human being. When it comes to speaking about God, human language is totally inadequate. Yet, although in one sense we cannot talk about God, we *have* to talk about God, while acknowledging that our talking about God never does justice to God. There is more to God that we can ever hope to put into words. At the same time, words are all we have.

Today's feast is the Feast of the Most Holy Trinity. Those words, 'Most Holy Trinity', are an effort to express an important truth about who God is. As Christians we believe that, although God is mysterious, Jesus is the fullest revelation of God possible in human form. In so far as God can be revealed at all in human form, Jesus is that self-revelation of God. If Jesus had not lived we would never have come to think of God as Trinity.

The Jews had a very strong conviction about the oneness of God. We find that expressed in today's first reading: 'The Lord is God indeed, he and no other.' The first Christians, who were Jews, shared that conviction. However, because of all that Jesus said and did, they came to recognise that within this oneness of God, there was a wonderful diversity. In other words, they understood that if God is one, he is one community. God's life is a communal life; within God there is the Father, the Son and the Holy Spirit who relate to each other in love. The church eventually came to speak of God as a Trinity of persons.

This is a very rich understanding of God and it is one that distinguishes Christianity from all other world religions. It has important implications for what human life is about. If in some way we are made in the image of God and if the life of God is a relational life of profound love, then our calling as human beings is to form loving relationships with others, to build community wherever we happen to find ourselves. We are most Godlike when we are in loving relationships with others, when we love others as God the Father loves Jesus and as Jesus has loved us, when our love for each other is the fruit of the Holy Spirit. Such loving and life-giving relationships are, therefore, a wonderful blessing; we are at our best when we are in them; they bring the best out in us.

Our calling is not only to build communities that reflect the community that is God. There is another dimension to our calling which is even more fundamental. We are invited into the communal life that is God; God draws us into God's own life. At the very beginning of our Christian life, we are baptised in the name of the Father, Son and Holy Spirit; we are baptised into the life of the Trinity. St Paul makes that clear in today's second reading. Through baptism we receive the Holy Spirit who makes us cry out, 'Abba, Father.' Through the Holy Spirit, God the Father unites us to God the Son, enables us to relate to God the Father in the way Jesus does, inspiring us to cry out 'Abba, Father' as Jesus does. It is extraordinary to think that we are invited to have the same relationship with God the Father that Jesus has, and that the Holy Spirit makes this possible. Even though God is very different from us, we are called into a very intimate relationship with God, Father, Son and Spirit.

It is in allowing ourselves to be drawn into the communal life of God in this way that we in turn will be enabled to build communities that reflect the life of God. In that sense, there is a twofold movement in our lives as Christians which is ongoing throughout our lives. We are continually drawn into the communal life of God and continually sent forth to form relationships that give expression to that life of God.

The Feast of Corpus Christi

We are all aware of the significance of tables in our lives. We all have our own memories of table fellowship. Many of those memories will be very happy. We remember celebration and laughter at tables, love given and received. Some of those memories of table fellowship may be sad. We might remember table experiences when we were more aware of the person who was absent than of those who were present.

Jesus shared table many times with his disciples. When sharing food with his disciples, Jesus also shared his vision of God's kingdom with them. At table, the disciples imbibed something of Jesus' mind and heart and spirit. Of all the meals Jesus shared with the disciples, the meal that stayed in their memory more than any other was the last meal they ate together, what came to be known as the last supper. Today's gospel gives us Mark's account of that last supper. Many great artists over the last two thousand years have attempted to express that moment on canvas, to paint it. This last meal Jesus shared with his disciples stood out in their memory, and captured the imagination of subsequent generations of disciples, because of what Jesus said and did at that meal. He did more than share his vision with the disciples; he did more than give them teaching. He gave them himself in a way he had never done before, in a way that anticipated the death he would die for them and for all, on the following afternoon. In giving the disciples himself in the form of the bread and wine of the meal, he was declaring himself to be their food and drink. In calling on them to take and eat, to take and drink, he was asking them to take their stand with him, to give themselves to him as he was giving himself to them.

It was because of that last supper and of what went on there that we are here in this church today. Jesus intended his last supper to be a beginning rather than an end. The last supper was the first Eucharist. Ever since that night, in response to Jesus' command, the church has gathered in his name, and has done and said what he did and said at that last supper. In this way, Jesus continues to give himself as food and drink to his followers. He also continues to put it up to his followers to take their stand with him, to take in all he stands for, living by his values, walking in his way, even if that means the cross. Whenever we come to Mass and receive the Eucharist, we are making a number of important statements. We are acknowledging Jesus as our bread of life, as the one who alone can satisfy our deepest hungers. We are also declaring that we will throw in our lot with him, as it were, that we will follow in his way and be faithful to him all our lives, in response to his faithfulness to us. In that sense, celebrating the Eucharist is not something we do lightly. Our familiarity with the Mass and the frequency with which we celebrate it can dull our senses to the full significance of what we are doing. Every time we gather to celebrate the Eucharist, we find ourselves once more in that upper room with the first disciples, and the last supper with all it signified is present again to us.

The last supper must have had a tremendously unifying effect on the disciples. In living through that last supper together they became conscious in a new way that they belonged not only to the Lord but also to each other. In a similar way, our weekly celebration of the Eucharist can and must have a bonding effect on ourselves. As St Paul says in one of his letters: 'We who are many are one body, for we all partake of the one bread.' As together we take the body of Christ and eat, we become more aware of ourselves as members of one body, the body of Christ. Our celebration of the Eucharist inspires us, and obliges us, to relate to each other as members of one body, Christ's body, Corpus Christi.

At this Eucharist, we commit ourselves again to living as members of the body of Christ. St Paul spells out what that means in practice. He says that the members of Christ's body are to 'have the same care for one another. If one member suffers, all suffer together with it; if one member is honoured, all rejoice together with it.' On this feast of the Body and Blood of Christ, here is a vision of church worth reminding ourselves of and recommitting ourselves to.

Second Sunday in Ordinary Time

When I was a child my parents were interested in who I mixed and played with. They were obviously convinced that some children of our own age would be more likely to lead us astray than others. They were of a generation who believed that who you mixed with helped to shape the person you would become. There is no doubt that we influence each other for good or for bad. Children are more susceptible to being influenced by others than adults are.

Many of us could think of people who influenced us for good at crucial moments in our lives. At a time when we were search-ing, without always knowing what we were searching for, they pointed us in the right direction. These people related to us with our best interests at heart. They served as a guide at a time when we needed direction. For many of us, our parents would have played such a role in our lives, and perhaps also a teacher, a col-league at work or a good friend.

Today's readings put before us a number of such people who were good guides to others. Eli was such a person for Samuel. The boy Samuel knew he was being called but he had no idea who was calling him. The elderly Eli came to realise that it was God who was calling and he helped Samuel to make an appro-priate response to God's call. Because of Eli's timely interven-tion, Samuel went on to become one of the great leaders of Israel. The older generation often have a great deal to offer the younger generation, especially when it comes to discerning what might be the best path to take in life, which path God may be calling us to take. Those who have lived most of their earthly life can often see more clearly than those at the beginning of their life. Grandparents can be a hugely influential presence for good in the lives of children.

The gospel reading presents us with another such guide in the person of John the Baptist. When John saw Jesus passing, he pointed his disciples in the direction of Jesus with the words: 'Look, there is the Lamb of God.' No doubt John had built up a relationship with his disciples, yet, clearly, it was in so sense a possessive relationship. John was prepared to part with his dis-ciples when someone came along whom John knew to be his better. As John would later say of Jesus: 'He must increase but I must decrease.' We might have known a John the Baptist in our own lives, a teacher or a mentor of some kind who, rather than holding on to us, helped us to move on, directed us to someone who had more to offer us than they themselves could offer us. There is a real self-emptying in performing that kind of service for someone. Letting go can sometimes be the most eloquent expression of love.

There is a second person in the gospel reading who shows himself to be a true guide to someone else. Andrew left his teacher John the Baptist and went to Jesus. As a result of his initial encounter with Jesus, Andrew in turn went to his brother Simon and brought Simon to Jesus. The age difference between Andrew and Simon would have been very slight. They were siblings, equals in terms of their experience of life. Yet, what John had been for Andrew, Andrew was for Simon. Good guides do not always have to be older than us; neither do they always have to be people who know more than we do or have lived more than we have. Andrew found a truly special person and he wanted to share that person with his brother. We often hear about sibling rivalry. There is no evidence of such rivalry in the case of these two brothers. Today's society can encourage us to see our peers as our competitors. The gospel encourages us to see them as fellow travellers. Sharing some treasure with someone who is our peer will never result in any loss to ourselves. It is in giving that we receive.

Eli, John the Baptist and Andrew all had one thing in common. They enabled others to grow spiritually. They helped others to grow in their relationship with the Lord. Later on in John's gospel, the Samaritan woman did the same for her townspeople. We are all called to perform this same service for each other. We do not journey to God on our own. We need each other's generous witness if we are to find and take the path God is calling us to take. Today's readings invite us to become an Eli or a John the Baptist or an Andrew for others.

Third Sunday in Ordinary Time

We can all become rather set in our ways. We get into certain ways of doing things and it can be tempting to stay with those ways and difficult to change from them. We develop routines and those routines keep us going. It often takes someone else to broaden our horizons a little, to open us up to areas of life that we would never otherwise have ventured into. We each might be able to identify such people in our own lives, those who introduced us to a set of experiences that proved to be very enriching and that helped us to grow as human beings.

We have a very striking example of that in today's gospel reading. Peter, Andrew, James and John lived in a world that was very much defined by the Sea of Galilee. They were fishermen and their lives revolved around that inland sea. They had every reason to believe that this would always be their way of life. Then, someone entered their lives and opened up a whole new horizon for them. The impact this man had on them was such that they left boats, nets, even family, to follow this man and to share in his mission. 'Follow me and I will make you fishers of people', Jesus had said to them. Instead of bringing fish to land, they would now share in Jesus' work of bringing people to God. Instead of shaping fishing nets, they would now shape lives. But, first, their own lives had to be shaped. They needed to spend time with Jesus, to learn from him and become like him, before they could share in his mission. It is hard to imagine a greater transformation in human lives than the one which today's gospel reading puts before us.

Jesus did not call everyone he met to the same radical change of lifestyle that we read about in today's gospel reading. Yet, all those who were receptive to him experienced a call to change in some way. If the call 'Follow me and I will make you fishers of people' was not addressed to everyone, the more fundamental call of Jesus that we hear in today's gospel reading was addressed to everyone: 'Repent and believe in the gospel.' This was fundamentally a call to change for the better, a call to turn more fully towards God who was present in a unique way in the person and life of Jesus. This is the call that is addressed to all of us. No matter where we find ourselves on life's journey, the risen Lord continues to address that fundamental call to each of us: 'Repent and believe the good news.' Because that call is addressed to each of us, it is also unique to each of us, and it will have a unique meaning for each of us. This Sunday is a good day to ask ourselves what this fundamental call of the Lord might mean for me personally.

The call of Jesus was not simply a call to repent. This was the call of John the Baptist. The more basic element of Jesus' call was 'believe the good news'. Jesus first announced this good news before he called on people to believe in it: 'The time has come, and the kingdom of God is at hand.' Jesus was declaring that through himself God was present to us in a life-giving way; this is the good news we are to believe. If God is present, then the first step is to joyfully acknowledge God's presence. This turning towards God present to us in Jesus comes first; the turning away from sin, repentance, follows on from that.

Jesus' declaration of the good news of God's life-giving and loving presence and his call to believe in that proclamation is what is most fundamental in our religion. Everything else is secondary, and is in some sense a working out of it. If we loose touch with this basic proclamation and call of Jesus, all the other elements of our faith will not make any sense. If we took Jesus' proclamation and call fully to heart, it would change us. Christians are asked to believe that at the core of life is good news, not bad news. If we believe that life is essentially bad news, then this conviction will shape all we do. The likelihood is that we will not be pleasant people to be around. If, however, we believe that at the heart of life is the life-giving and loving presence of a personal God who calls out to us through his Son, then how we relate, how we behave, will be very different indeed. Today's gospel brings us back to basics, and if we get the basics right the rest will follow.

Fourth Sunday in Ordinary Time

Most of us can think back on times when we did or said some-thing that we subsequently regretted. When we look back on such times we often ask ourselves how we could have done or said such a thing. We might find ourselves saying: 'I don't know what got into me' or 'I was not myself at the time.' We are thereby acknowledging that it was not our true self that found expres-sion on that occasion. Looking back, we may sense that some spirit or other got into us and made us act or speak out of charac-ter, in a way that we subsequently regretted and even disowned. Thankfully, as a general rule, such spirits only take hold of us momentarily. We may be aware that we have our demons but most of the time they do not dominate us. Every so often they may break through in ways that leave us embarrassed and re-gretful.

In the gospel reading this morning, we hear the story of a man who was possessed by an unclean spirit. Some spirit had taken hold of him, not momentarily, but in an enduring way. He was permanently possessed by this spirit. It made him address Jesus in very aggressive tones: 'What do you want with us, Jesus of Nazareth? Have you come to destroy us?' Jesus knew that the voice of the spirit speaking through this man was not the man's real voice. He was aware that it was not the man's true self that he was encountering. Jesus set about the work of healing this man and delivering him from this alien spirit. Jesus restored his true self.

What Jesus did for this man he can do for all of us. The same Jesus who spoke with authority in the synagogue of Capernaum is alive among us as risen Lord. The powerful, life-giving word that Jesus addressed to that man he continues to address to each of us. The crowd on that occasion said: 'Here is a teaching that is new and with authority behind it.' The word of Jesus has lost none of its newness or its authority. It is a word that remains alive today. Jesus continues to address his word to us today, and that word has the power to deliver us from those spirits that diminish us. Jesus' opening words to the man were: 'Be quiet.' They might well be his first words to us as well. We need to be quiet if we are to be touched by the Lord's word. We need to find some stillness if the Lord's word is to make the same kind of impact on us as it made on the man in today's gospel reading. That stillness may take the form of a few quiet moments after Mass sitting with the Lord's word to us in the readings. As we sit in stillness we name those unclean spirits in our lives that prevent us from being our best self, and we ask the Lord to speak with authority for our healing and our liberation.

What the Lord did for that man and what he can do for us, he calls on us to do for one another. He speaks his life-giving word into our lives so that we can speak that same word into each other's lives. We know only too well that the words we speak can be forces for good or forces for harm. Some words can leave deep wounds and other words can heal and renew. Some words can give our demons a new lease of life and other words disempower our demons. Words do matter, both what we say and how we say it. It is true that actions speak louder than words, but words themselves are actions in their own right; they do something. The authoritative word of Jesus in today's gospel reading did something wonderful; it brought healing and new life to a very disturbed person. Today's gospel reading might prompt us to look at what our own words do.

Jesus' words came from the depth of his relationship with God. That is why they were such a power for good. As followers of Jesus, our words are to come from the depth of our relationship with him. Only then will they share in the power for good that his words had. Sometimes our words come from a more superficial place; they might be a reaction to the careless words that are spoken to us. Jesus did not just react to the hostile words that were spoken to him in today's gospel reading; his words came from a deeper place. Our calling is to allow our words to come from that same deeper place so that they will have the same power for good that his words had.

Fifth Sunday in Ordinary Time

One of the very sad and tragic features of the time in which we live is the number of people who take their own lives. Men in early adulthood seem to be a particularly vulnerable group. It is difficult to understand the bleakness of spirit that must be at the root of such a drastic step. Bleakness of spirit can afflict all of us. There can be many reasons for such bleakness of spirit. Our life can take a turn for the worst for one reason or another. Something deeply distressing can happen to us or to someone with whom we are very close. It is at such times that the words of Job in today's first reading find a ready echo in our hearts: 'Is not our life on earth nothing more than pressed service, our time no better than hired drudgery?' These are the words of one who has a sense of hopelessness in the face of the darkness of life.

What saved Job from total despair is that he was able to express how he felt to God. He addressed God very directly, sometimes in very angry and uncompromising terms. A few verses after our reading, he bellows at God: 'Will you not look away from me for a while; let me alone until I swallow my spittle.' Job had enough freedom in his relationship with God to speak to God directly out of the darkness of his experience. Job teaches us to speak to God out of the depths. The old Catechism definition of prayer that I learned at school was: 'Prayer is the raising up of the mind and heart to God.' If prayer is the raising up of the mind and heart to God, then prayer is the raising up of everything that is in our mind and heart to God. If what is in our minds and hearts are the darkest of human sentiments and thoughts, then that is what we must raise up to God. We speak to God out of the reality of our lives, whatever that reality might be. Job shows us that our prayer does not have to be censured. If prayer is not real, it is not really prayer.

There is a line in today's responsorial psalm which states: 'The Lord heals the broken-hearted.' As Job continued at length to speak to God out of his broken heart, he eventually went on to find healing. Jesus revealed God to be close to the broken, to those who were broken in body, mind, spirit or heart. The gospel reading this morning shows the closeness of Jesus and, therefore, of God, to the broken. Indeed, in Jesus, God became one of the broken. On the cross Jesus reveals a God who is broken in body and spirit. God entered our brokenness in Jesus, and experienced it from the inside. God could not get closer to the broken than that.

In today's second reading, St Paul says of himself: 'For the weak, I made myself weak.' God could say the very same: 'For the weak I made myself weak; for the broken, I made myself broken.' If that is the God in whom we believe, then we need have no hesitation in bringing our brokenness to God in prayer. Many of us will be familiar with the saying: 'A burden shared is a burden halved.' Sometimes it can be difficult to share our burden with another, even with the person we are closest to. If we cannot share a burden with our closest companion, it is not the case that the only alternative is to keep it to ourselves. We can share that burden with the Lord. The prayer of sharing, the prayer of the open heart, is a very authentic form of prayer. Sharing ourselves with God in this way is not quite the same as asking God for something, petitioning God. We are simply sharing; we are telling our story to God, opening up that story to God's presence, to God's influence.

In today's gospel reading, we find Jesus at prayer. He had been ministering to the broken most of the day. Early next morning, he got up and went off to a lonely place and prayed there. Working with the burdened no doubt left him burdened, as is the case for all of us. His prayer was a time to share his burden with the Father. In doing so, he found strength to continue. 'Let us go elsewhere, to the neighbouring country towns', he said to his disciples after his prayer. The best teaching is often by example. Jesus is teaching us here by his own example to lift up whatever may be in our hearts and minds to God and in doing that to find new strength.

Sixth Sunday in Ordinary Time

We know from experience that we find it easier to connect with some people than with others. We find ourselves drawn to some individuals and being somewhat put off by others. We can react negatively to some people for a great variety of reasons. Maybe we just do not like the look of them, or we find their personality hard to take, or we have very little sympathy with their views. We probably tend to avoid the people that we find difficult to connect with. We keep them at a distance from us.

In the time of Jesus the leper was someone that no one wanted to connect with. Indeed, the Jewish law required that lepers be kept at a distance from everyone else. Leprosy was a disease that condemned those afflicted by it to a life in which their only company was other lepers. The disease was contagious and the community had to be preserved from infection. In today's gospel reading the leper leaves his isolation and daringly approaches Jesus, calling out to him on his knees: 'If you want to, you can cure me.' He was prepared to break the law that condemned him to isolation in order to make contact with Jesus. Clearly the leper did not doubt Jesus' ability to heal him: 'You can cure me.' His only doubt was whether Jesus wanted to cure him, 'if you want to'. In response to the leper, Jesus did the unthinkable. He stretched out his hand and touched him, declaring as he did so: 'Of course, I want to!' The man could now return to the community from which he had been isolated. In connecting with the leper, Jesus enabled the leper to connect with everyone else. In touching him, he enabled the leper to touch others.

In touching the leper, Jesus reveals a God who wants to make contact with us in all our brokenness. Jesus was declaring that there is no human life that God cannot touch. Everyone kept a distance from the leper. In touching the leper, Jesus was declaring that God is not like everyone. We may keep our distance from God for various reasons, but God never keeps a distance from us. We may think that because of something we have done in the past, we cannot approach God with confidence. Jesus reveals that God is always ready to approach us, regardless of how we might see ourselves, or how others might see us. Jesus could have healed the leper without touching him. The gospel

78

often depicts Jesus healing people with a word. Yet, in the case of the leper, word was not enough. Touching the leper was a much more tangible sign that God wanted to connect with this man. Jesus makes God tangible as well as audible.

God continues to be tangible as well as audible in the church, the body of the risen Jesus. There is more to the sacraments of the church than words. The sacraments are tangible; they reveal the God who wants to touch us. The water of baptism, the oil of confirmation, the bread and wine of the Eucharist are all tangible signs of God's presence to us. God wants to touch our lives through his Son. If it does nothing else, the story of Jesus and the leper makes that abundantly clear. The only question is: 'Do we want God to touch our lives?' When it comes to God, do we have the passionate daring that the leper shows in today's gospel reading?

Outside the context of family and close friends, we have to be careful with touch nowadays. In particular, many of us are much more hesitant to touch children than we might have been in the past. We know that touch can mean many things. It can be self-serving as well as serving of others. It can be harmful as well as helpful. In the culture of his time, Jesus seemed to be remarkably free when it came to touch. In last Sunday's gospel reading, he took Simon Peter's mother in law by the hand and lifted her up; later on in Mark's gospel he takes Jairus' daughter by the hand and he takes children up in his arms and lays his hands on them. We are hesitant when it comes to touch because we know of what we are made. Jesus had no need to be hesitant. His touch was always deeply respectful and completely life-giving. Jesus shows us a God who recognises our infinite value and worth and relates to us accordingly. That is why in the words of the letter to the Hebrews, we can 'approach the throne of grace with confidence, so that we may receive mercy and find grace to help us in our time of need'.

Seventh Sunday in Ordinary Time

We all value our independence. We like to feel that we can take our own initiatives and follow through on them. We do not like to think of ourselves as a burden on others. Yet, no matter how independent we are, there comes a time in all our lives when we simply cannot go it alone, when we need help and support from others. For many of us, this will be during a time of illness. When we are ill, there are some things we simply cannot do for ourselves. We need others to do them for us. It may be as simple as needing someone to do some shopping because we are confined to the house. Here, good neighbours can be a wonderful resource. We seem to have retreated more into our own private spaces in recent years. If that were to become more prominent, we stand to loose a great deal. The fact is there will always come a time when we need each other. Elderly people living alone, in particular, who may not have much in the way of family, need good neighbours.

Today's gospel reading gives us a very striking picture of the human need of others in a time of sickness. A paralytic is carried to Jesus by four friends, four neighbours more than likely. The four men in today's gospel reading were passionately committed to their friend. We can almost hear them saying: 'If we cannot get him through the crowd, we will just have to get him through the roof.' I suspect the phrase, 'It can't be done', was not part of their vocabulary. They had a goal in view: Get this man to Jesus. They were going to make that happen. When Jesus saw what these four men were prepared to do for their friend, he recognised that the driving force of their efforts was their faith in him. 'Seeing their faith, Jesus said to the paralytic …' It was the faith of the four friends rather than the faith of the paralytic himself that Jesus recognised. The paralytic was carried to Jesus by the faith of these four men. Whether the paralytic himself was a man of faith, we are not told.

The picture the gospel reading gives us of the paralysed man being carried by the faith of others is an image of the church. In times of difficulty and struggle, our own faith can grow weak. When some misfortune hits us, we may find ourselves wondering if God has abandoned us, or we may discover a certain amount of anger in us towards God. We may find it very diffi-cult to pray in the ways we have been used to praying. A dark-ness of spirit can come over us. At such times when we struggle for faith within ourselves, the faith of others can help to carry us. We may not be able to pray, but to be told by others that they are praying for us can be a great comfort. As a church, we are a fam-ily of faith, a body of faith, the body of Christ, the faithful one. When the faith of one member grows week, the faith of others can compensate. There comes a time when we all need the faith of others to keep us going. There is a very real sense in which we carry each other to the Lord. Sometimes we will be among the carriers; at other times we will be among those being carried. As we began life, we were carried to the Lord by the faith of others. The faith of our parents and grandparents brought us to the bap-tismal font at a time when we had no faith ourselves. The flame of their faith burned for us. As we grow beyond childhood into adulthood we will often be called upon to keep the flame of faith burning for others. There will also be times, however, when as adults our faith will grow weak and we will look to others to keep the flame of faith burning for us.

Although our faith, our 'yes' to God, can grow weak, Paul as-sures us in today's second reading that Christ Jesus is never 'yes' and 'no'. Rather, with him it is always 'yes'. All of God's promis-es to us find their 'yes' in him. If we are carried at times by the faith of others, in a more fundamental sense we are carried by the Lord's own faith. St. Paul in his letter to the Romans speaks of Christ Jesus 'who was raised, who is at the right hand of God, who, indeed, intercedes for us'. It is reassuring to know that when we cannot pray, the risen Lord is praying for us. When our faith in him grows weak, his faith in us remains strong.

Eighth Sunday in Ordinary Time

One of the signs of the times today is the speed of communication. The great symbol of that is the e-mail. You can e-mail someone in another hemisphere and they can reply, all in a matter of minutes. For all its value, the e-mail is unlikely to totally eclipse the letter. From time to time, we will still feel the need to write a letter, even to those for whom we have an e-mail address. We sense that a letter written to someone in our own handwriting is experienced by them as a more personal communication from us.

St Paul knew all about writing letters. He was a great letter writer. We read a section of his second letter to the Corinthians this morning. In that reading he uses a striking image. He tells the members of the church in Corinth that they themselves are a letter written by Christ and that he, Paul, is the secretary that Christ used in writing this letter. This letter was written by Christ on their hearts through Paul by means of the Holy Spirit. Paul was reminding the Corinthians that they are Christ's letter to the world, that their lives are a message from Christ to be seen and read by all.

It is thought-provoking to think of our own lives as letters. That image may be in the background when we say of someone that 'he/she is a difficult person to read' or when we say 'you can read him/her like a book'. Paul's words to the Corinthians might prompt us to ask ourselves: 'How do people read us?' 'What message is my way of life sending out to others?' Paul is suggesting that we become a letter from Christ, that we allow the Lord to write the script of our lives. In that way, we become not just people who have a message but people whose lives are a message, Christ's message. The Lord through the Holy Spirit seeks to write a letter with our lives, a letter that proclaims his loving presence to others. If we are open to the movement of the Holy Spirit within us, the Lord's letter will get written in and through our lives, and the lives of those with whom we are in contact will be all the richer.

Once we have sent a letter, it is gone. We can't change it. The most we can do is to send another letter correcting the one we have sent. It is not always wise to send the letter we have written.

A person who was very angry with someone wrote a very strong letter to that person. Fortunately, he first showed it to a friend before sending it. The friend said: 'It is a fine letter. It was good for you to write it. Now, tear it up and write another one.' We need to be careful what we write because words on a page cannot change. However, that is not true of our lives. If our lives are letters, they are letters that are always open to change. We need never say of our lives: 'What I have written, I have written.' Our past or present script need not be the final script of our lives, at least not in the Lord's eyes. Yet, we can be tempted to hold onto one particular script for our own lives. We can forget that the Lord never ceases to work on the letter that is our lives. In that sense, our lives are always an evolving letter, one that will only be truly finished when our names are written in heaven.

In the gospel reading this morning, Jesus encounters people who are holding on strongly to one particular script, both for their own lives and the lives of others. When Jesus and his disciples were attempting to write a different script to the one they were used to, they ask 'Why?' in a somewhat accusing fashion. In the image of the gospel reading, they were clinging to old wine skins at a time when Jesus was doing something new that cried out for new wine skins. In the first reading also, the prophet announces to the people of Israel that God was about to do something new in their lives. They were not to live in exile forever; the experience of exile would not be the final chapter of their lives. God would lead them out of exile into the wilderness where the marriage bond between them and God would be renewed, and then God would finally lead them home. God continues to work in all our lives in new and creative ways. There is always a new chapter in our lives that God through his Son stands ready to write, regardless of how old we are.

Ninth Sunday in Ordinary Time

We tend to put valuables in places that are secure. We place treasures in banks and vaults. The more valuable an item is, the more careful we are to see that it is guarded. Paul's comment in today's second reading seems to fly in the face of such conventional wisdom: 'We are only the earthenware jars that hold this treasure.' The 'treasure' Paul was referring to was the treasure of the gospel, what he had referred to a few verses earlier as 'the light of the gospel of the glory of Christ who is the image of God'. The Creator God who brought light out of darkness has enlightened our minds and hearts with this light of the gospel, 'the light of the knowledge of God's glory, the glory on the face of Christ', in the words of today's reading. Yet, Paul is very aware that we who have been given this treasure are only earthenware jars. In Paul's time, such jars were used to hold the oil that enabled a wick placed in the jar to remain lighting once it was lit. Earthenware jars were prone to breaking; they were very vulnerable. If knocked over, they would smash on any hard surface. Fortunately, they were inexpensive and could easily be replaced when broken.

Paul was aware of the paradox at the heart of every believer. We have been entrusted with a wonderful treasure in the gospel, one that is capable of shedding God's light on all who are open to receiving it. We who have been given this treasure, however, are brittle and vulnerable; we are prone to brokenness of various kinds, whether it is brokenness of body, mind or spirit. The Lord's ways are not our ways. Whereas we place our treasures in the strongest possible container, the Lord has entrusted his treasure to those who are weak and frail. The Lord has taken a risk that we would be very slow to take. Yet, as Paul reminds us in our reading, our weakness and frailty only serves to show forth more clearly the power of the treasure we have been given, the power of the gospel. The power of the gospel is God's power, the power of God's love seeking us out through the life, death and resurrection of Christ. In our weakness and brokenness, we can draw healing and strength from that power for ourselves, while becoming channels of that loving and life-giving power to others.

Jesus was himself an earthenware jar. He entered fully into the weakness and vulnerability of the human condition. He would end up broken on a Roman cross. More than any other human being, he contained within himself the treasure of the gospel. Indeed, more than that, he is the treasure of the gospel; he is the pearl of great price. He embodies in himself the power of the gospel, the power of God's life-giving love. The gospel reading this morning shows this power at work in and through Jesus. On entering a synagogue, he meets with a man who had a withered hand. The power of God's love present in Jesus heals this man's brokenness. The treasure of the gospel, alive in Jesus, brings light where there is darkness, strength where there is weakness, wholeness where there is brokenness. The one who, in the words of Paul, would be 'crucified in weakness' demonstrates the power of God's life-giving love.

Because we have been entrusted with the same treasure of the gospel, we too can share in the Lord's life-giving ministry, vulnerable and weak as we are. There is much that is withered in our world. We encounter withered bodies, withered spirits, withered hopes, withered hearts and, sometimes, withered communities and withered institutions. If we value the gospel as our primary treasure and allow that gospel to take hold of us and to shape us, the power of the gospel working through us will continue to renew and transform what is withered. We can never underestimate the power of the gospel in our feeble hands, because, in the words of the letter to the Ephesians, God's 'power at work within us is able to accomplish abundantly far more than all we can ask or imagine'.

Yet, the gospel reading this morning shows us that the treasure of the gospel will not always be well received. When Jesus allowed the hungry to satisfy their hunger on the Sabbath by taking from the fruits of God's creation, he was sharply criticized. When he went further and brought healing and life on the Sabbath to one who was withered, some began to discuss how they might destroy him. The treasure of the gospel we carry within us will not always be well received, but that does not make it any less of a treasure.

Tenth Sunday in Ordinary Time

We can all be prone to misjudging people. We see someone behave in a certain way and we draw certain conclusions from it that are not warranted. We can make certain assessments of others on the basis of how they appear and we get our assessment completely wrong. Our insight into others can be quite limited. This is not necessarily a problem as long as we recognise that our insight is indeed limited and that we are open to modifying that insight on the basis of further experience and information.

In this morning's gospel reading, Jesus' family showed a somewhat limited insight into who he was and what he was doing. Because of the pace at which he was working and the hostility he was bringing on himself from the religious leaders, his family were accepting the judgement of others that Jesus was out of his mind. He was acting outside acceptable norms and he needed to be taken in hand. The religious leaders, in their growing hostility to Jesus, showed an even greater misjudgement as to who Jesus was and what he was doing. They had concluded that he was healing people through the power of Satan. The power that was at work within him, even though its fruits appeared to be good, was a demonic power and not a divine power. There was a great gulf between who Jesus was in reality and what Jesus' family and, especially, the scribes saw when they looked upon Jesus.

In today's second reading, Paul also draws attention to this gap between appearance and reality. With reference to himself, he declares that 'though this outer man of ours may be falling into decay, the inner man is renewed day by day'. By the time Paul wrote the second letter to the Corinthians, he had endured a great deal for the sake of the gospel. Towards the beginning of the letter he refers to a very recent experience, speaking of 'the affliction we experienced in Asia' and stating that 'we were so utterly, unbearable crushed that we despaired of life itself'. To an external observer, Paul must have seemed a failure and a loser. Yet, in spite of his hardships and losses for the sake of the gospel, Paul's inner spirit was being renewed day by day. A little later in that letter he speaks of 'having nothing, yet possessing everything'. His relationship with Christ is the one thing that could not be taken from him, and because of this relationship he possessed everything, regardless of the often dire circumstances of his life. How Paul was in reality was very different from how he was perceived by others, especially his opponents.

Both Jesus and Paul teach us that there is often a great deal more to each of us than others give us credit for. Even members of our own families can sell us short by the way they perceive us and relate to us. Neither Jesus nor Paul allowed themselves to be defined by how others saw them. Their sense of who they were came not so much from the way others related to them but from how God related to them. Jesus knew that even though the scribes saw him as a servant of Satan, God saw him as his own beloved Son. It was God's perception of him which determined how Jesus lived and worked.

How God relates to us is of much greater significance in determining who we really are than how others relate to us. According to the gospel reading, God relates to the followers of his Son as members of his new family. Jesus declares to his disciples, those sitting around him in a circle listening to his teaching, that they are his brothers and sisters and, therefore, sons and daughters of God. Through baptism, God has sent the Spirit of his Son into our hearts, crying 'Abba, Father'. We have been taken up into Jesus' own relationship with God. God now relates to us as God relates to his only Son. Because of that God has destined us to inherit the fullness of life that Jesus now enjoys. In today's second reading, Paul refers to what awaits us beyond this life as a 'weight of eternal glory which is out of all proportion' to the troubles that afflict us in this life. The sense of who we are in God's eyes and who we are destined to become can give us courage and confidence, even in those times when the way others relate to us leaves a lot to be desired. As Paul declares: 'I believe and therefore I speak – we too believe and therefore we speak.' Jesus exemplifies such confidence in today's gospel reading in the way he speaks up against those who would devalue and demonise him.

Eleventh Sunday in Ordinary Time

Children at a certain age are great for asking questions. They ask one question and, having received an answer, they ask another question on the basis of the second answer. As children grow into adolescence, they begin to ask more probing questions, questions that look for some kind of light to be cast on the deeper issues of life. In time, they may come to realise that clear answers are not always to be found to life's more profound questions. As adults we often have to reconcile ourselves to living with many unanswered questions. We discover that all our searching will never exhaust the many mysteries of life. We continue to take delight in making fresh discoveries, but we also realise that coming to terms with 'not knowing' is an important part of life's journey.

In this morning's gospel reading, Jesus speaks a parable which acknowledges the mystery that is at the heart of the most everyday experiences of life. A farmer scatters seed on the good soil of Galilee. Having done his job, he can only go about his other business, while the seed takes over and does its own work, producing first the shoot, then the ear, then the full grain in the ear, until the crop is ready for harvest. In the parable it is said of the farmer that 'he does not know' how all this happens. Between his actions of sowing the seed and harvesting the crop, a great deal of activity goes on, which is invisible to him and which he does not understand. There is a great deal in our physical universe which we still do not fully understand, in spite of the great expertise that has developed over the centuries on all aspects of our earth and our universe.

In speaking that parable, Jesus was not just talking about farmers and seeds and the natural growth process. He begins the parable with the statement: 'This is what the kingdom of God is like.' If the farmer does not know the ways of the humble seed, how can any of us fully know the ways of God? If natural growth is mysterious, how much more must spiritual growth be mysterious? The author of the book of Qoheleth expressed it well: 'Just as you do not know how the breath comes to the bones in the mother's womb, so you do not know the work of God, who makes everything.' By means of this parable, Jesus was making a much more positive statement than that the ways of God are mysterious. He appears to be saying that the kingdom of God is growing among you in ways that you do not understand, just as the seed the farmer sows in the ground grows towards harvest in ways he does not understand. There is an encouraging, hopeful message here for disciples who may be tempted to discouragement by the slow progress that the way of God appears to be making in the world. The coming of God's kingdom, the spreading of God's reign, is ultimately God's work and that work is always ongoing, even when we do not see it. We have a part to play in the coming to birth of God's way of doing things among us, but it is a limited part, just as the farmer has a limited role to play in the coming of the final harvest. We can both overestimate and underestimate our role in God's work. Today's parable warns us against overestimating our role. St Paul expresses this perspective well in his first letter to the Corinthians, using imagery that reflects the language of our parable: 'Neither the one who plants, nor the one who waters is anything, but only God who gives the growth.'

The second of the two parables that Jesus speaks in today's gospel reading reminds us that God can be hard at work in situations and in places that seem very unpromising to us. There is a stark contrast between the tiny mustard seed, 'the smallest of all the seeds on earth', and the large shrub whose branches become homes for the birds of the air. Insignificant beginnings can lead to a wonderful result. The parable assures us that God is as much at work in the insignificant beginnings as in the final product. We can feel at times that our own faith is insignificant, as small as a mustard seed. The parable assures us that the Lord is working in and through such faith. Our hope can appear to diminish to the size of a mustard seed. The parable assures us that such hope is enough for the Lord. Our worthwhile endeavours can appear to bear very insignificant results. The parable assures us that the Lord will ensure the final harvest from those endeavours will be abundant.

Twelfth Sunday in Ordinary Time

In these summer months many people head to the beach and swim in the sea. Some might be members of sailing clubs and will make the most of these days when the sea tends to be quieter. Ferries that sail across seas are less likely to be cancelled these months for reasons of bad weather. Yet, we know that the sea can be treacherous and can claim lives at any time of the year. Those who know the sea have learned to treat it with respect, whatever the season.

The Sea of Galilee which features in today's gospel reading is more a very large lake than a sea. Yet, because it is below sea level and surrounded by hills and valleys, winds can blow down the valleys and whip up those waters without much prior notice. Some of the disciples who were in the boat with Jesus were fishermen. They knew the lake well. When a storm broke on the lake, however, they were understandably filled with fear. Something of their panic is captured in the words they address to Jesus: 'Master, do you not care? We are going down.' The panic of the disciples stands in sharp contrast to the attitude of Jesus – 'in the stern, his head on a cushion, asleep'. The panic of the disciples revealed their anxiety that the chaos of the storm would overwhelm them; the sleep of Jesus indicated his deep conviction that all would be well.

Mark's gospel was probably written to the church in Rome about the year 70. It had experienced the trauma of Nero's persecution and, in the process, had lost many of its key leaders, such as Peter and Paul. Here was a deeply traumatised community which felt very insecure in a society that could unexpectedly and violently turn against them. As the members of the church tried to come to terms with their bruising experience, some of them may have been wondering, 'Where is the risen Lord in all of this?' Has he abandoned us? Is he asleep to what is happening to us? In including this incident in his gospel, Mark was trying to assure them that this was not the case. As Jesus was in the boat with the disciples when the storm broke, he is with the church in its ordeal. The implication in the disciples' question, 'Master, do you not care?' is unfounded. The risen Lord does care. The question the Lord put to those disciples was being put to the church of Mark's day: 'Why are you so frightened? How is it that you have no faith?' The disciples of Mark's own day are also being invited to reflect on the question of the disciples in the boat: 'Who can this be?' and to give the answer: 'Jesus is the one who brings order out of chaos, life out of death.'

This is also the answer that we, the church today, are being asked to give to this question. No one can deny that the church has been through some stormy times, with some of the storms of the church's own making. Recent years have been a disheartening time for many believers. The waves of secularism and materialism threaten to sink the church, which has often been understood as the ship of Peter. Such storms can have their own cathartic effect on the church; they can work to the church's good. The disciples in today's gospel reading undoubtedly learned something important from their traumatic experience on the Sea of Galilee. The storm made them question more deeply: 'Who then is this?' A weakened, vulnerable church can come to recognise in a new way its total dependence on the Lord. When all is not well, we learn to seek the Lord with greater passion, like the disciples in the boat, rather than presuming that we already know him. Difficult and painful times can deepen the church's relationship with the Lord.

In today's second reading, St Paul reflects on the relationship between the Lord and the church. He declares that Christ died for all so that we might live no longer for ourselves but for him. We who are the church do not live for ourselves, but for the Lord. The church exists to serve the Lord, not itself. The storms through which the church passes can help it to re-appropriate this fundamental truth. We all need something to live for. As baptised members of the church, we do not live for some*thing* but for some*one*. In all we say and do, we try to serve the Lord rather than ourselves, to promote his cause, his purpose, rather than our own. This is our goal in life, what today's gospel reading refers to as 'the other side' of the lake that we are always striving to reach.

Thirteenth Sunday in Ordinary Time

We know from our own experience how one community can be a great resource to another community that may be going through a difficult time. In the second reading today, Paul calls on the Christian community in Corinth to provide for another Christian community that could not provide for itself. The church in Jerusalem had limited material resources and had known famine in recent times. Paul called on the church in Corinth to place their present surplus at the service of the Jerusalem church's present need.

We are also aware that one individual can help another individual to get through a difficult period. Many of us may have found ourselves in the situation where we had to act on behalf of others who were in no position to act for themselves. We may have provided for sick children or infirm parents or friends who were immobilised for whatever reason. Our healthy legs were able to do for them what their weak legs could not do for themselves. Our resources of strength and energy compensated for their own lack of such resources. It is quite likely that many of us will have been in the reverse situation of needing others to do for us what we were unable to do for ourselves. It can be much more difficult to find ourselves in this role of needing help than in the role of giving help. Giving can come easier to us than receiving.

In today's gospel reading we find Jairus, the leader of the synagogue, placing all his resources of energy and love at the disposal of his dying daughter. She lay at home helpless. He would do all in his power to compensate for her helplessness. He took the initiative to seek out Jesus. He threw himself at Jesus' feet, pleading with him for his sick daughter. Jairus was a man who had a significant position of honour in his community. Such men did not throw themselves at other people's feet. In the culture of the time this would have been regarded as a very dishonourable action. Yet, his daughter's life meant much more to Jairus than his own reputation in the eyes of others. He acted as any parent would act whose child was in desperate need. Parents will risk their lives to save the life of their child. They will enter burning buildings to rescue their child, even though in the process they are endangering their own lives.

Just as there are times when we energetically give everything we have for those who matter most to us, there are other times when we need to be equally energetic about taking some initiative on our own behalf. We can find ourselves in certain situations where it is we ourselves who have to make the primary move. No one else can really do that for us. The woman with the flow of blood in today's gospel reading is a good example of someone who takes an initiative on her own behalf. She did not ask anyone to go to Jesus for her; she went to him herself. She showed great boldness in approaching Jesus in the way she did. In the religious culture of that time, a woman with her condition was expected to keep her distance from those who were considered holy, as Jesus was. The cultural expectations of the time did not undermine this woman's determination to make contact with Jesus – even if it was only to touch the hem of his cloak. Jesus went on to publicly acknowledge her great faith. Here was a faith that was on a par with that of Jairus who threw himself at Jesus' feet on behalf of his daughter.

If Jairus in the gospel reading and Paul in the second reading speak to us of our need to invest ourselves wholeheartedly in the care of those who are vulnerable, the woman in the gospel reading speaks to us of our need to invest ourselves in making contact with the Lord for ourselves and in growing in our relationship with him. Yes, the Lord seeks us out, but he looks to us to seek him out too. The energy that drove the woman to make contact with Jesus was her awareness that she could only be whole and complete in and through him. We too believe that it is only in relationship with him that we will become all that God is calling us to be. The first reading tells us that we were made in the image of God's own nature. Jesus was the full image of God. It is in reaching out to touch him and to engage with him, like the woman in the gospel reading, that we too will grow into the image of God that we were created to be.

Fourteenth Sunday in Ordinary Time

When family members leave home for the first time to make some kind of a home of their own it can be a very difficult experience for all the family. The one leaving will often have mixed feelings, wanting to strike out and become independent and yet feeling the pain of leaving loved ones. Parents will often have the same mixed feelings, happy that their son or daughter is ready to move on and yet knowing that they will miss them very much. In contrast to partings, homecomings are more likely to be very happy experiences. Yet, homecomings can also be complicated affairs. The one returning for a visit may have changed significantly since leaving home, and those at home may have changed too. There can be certain expectations all round that are more appropriate to how things were in the past than to how things have become in the meantime. Adjusting to the changes that have taken place while the family member was away can be a challenge for everyone.

In today's gospel reading, Jesus returns to his home town of Nazareth, having left there some time previously. He had spent the best part of thirty years in Nazareth. During that time he was known by all as the carpenter, the son of Mary. However, in the time since he left Nazareth, Jesus' life had taken a new direction. He had thrown himself into the work that God had given him to do. He had left Nazareth as a carpenter; he returned to Nazareth as a teacher and a healer. There was in fact much more to this man that his own townspeople had ever suspected while he was living among them. The gospel reading suggests that they could not accept this 'more'. They wanted him to be the person they had always known, the carpenter. Jesus' homecoming turned out to be more painful than his leaving home. The one sent to proclaim the presence of God's kingdom was despised among his own relations and in his own house and rejected by them.

The people of Nazareth thought they knew Jesus. The image they had of him, which they held on to with great tenacity, became a block to their learning more about him. It was Jesus' very ordinariness that made it difficult for the people of Nazareth to see him as God saw him, in all his mystery. God was powerfully present to them in and through someone who was as ordinary,

in many respects, as they themselves. God continues to come to us today in and through the ordinary, in and through those who are most familiar to us. In the religious sphere there can be a certain fascination with the extraordinary and the unusual. The gospels suggest, however, that the primary way the Lord comes to us is in and through the everyday. This is what we mean by the incarnation. The Word became flesh and dwelt among us. The ordinary is shot through with God's presence. The burning bush that fascinated Moses is everywhere.

The Lord can even come to us in and through what we initially experience as something very negative. St Paul made this discovery for himself, according to our second reading today. He struggled with what he called a 'thorn in the flesh'. It is not easy to know what he means by this. It could refer to some physical ailment or to some person. Whatever it was, Paul wanted to be rid of it. He saw no good in it and he prayed earnestly to the Lord to take it from him, fully expecting that his prayer would be heard. Paul's prayer was answered, but not in the way he had expected. In prayer he came to realise that God was powerfully present in and through this thorn in the flesh that he had come to consider an instrument of Satan.

When we find ourselves struggling with something inside ourselves or with something outside ourselves, some person perhaps, we can be tempted to see the struggle as totally negative and just want to be rid of it. Like Paul, however, we can discover that this 'thorn in the flesh' is opening us up to God's presence. The very thing we judge to be of little or no value can create a space for God to work powerfully in our lives. There is something of a paradox in what Paul hears the risen Lord say to him: 'My power is at its best in weakness.' Indeed, God worked most powerfully not through the wisdom and the miracles of Christ but through the weakness of his passion and death. It is often when we most feel life as a struggle that God can touch our lives most powerfully and creatively.

Fifteenth Sunday in Ordinary Time

The months of July and August are traditionally the months when people take holidays. More often than not we speak in terms of going on holiday. For most of us, a holiday involves setting out on a journey of some kind. An important part of a holiday is leaving the place where we usually live and work and heading off to a different kind of place. There is always something exciting about setting out on such a journey. We make such a journey gladly and willingly, with a sense of expectation and anticipation. Such journeys are of our own choosing; we make them because we want to make them.

There are other journeys in life we find ourselves making that are not of our choosing in quite the same way. These are journeys we make because, at some level, we feel we must make them. Something deep within us moves us to take a certain path, to head out in a certain direction. Even though we sense the journey may be difficult, nonetheless we know that we have to set out on this path, if we are to be true to ourselves. Yes, we choose to make such a journey, but it is a choice in response to what seems like a call from beyond ourselves or from deep within ourselves.

Such a journey is put before us in today's first reading. Amos was a shepherd and a dresser of sycamore trees in the southern kingdom of Judah. Yet, at a certain moment in his life, he felt under compulsion to make a difficult journey into the northern kingdom of Israel to preach the word of God. It was a most unlikely journey for the likes of Amos to make, and Amos was well aware that it would be no holiday. Yet, he also knew that this was a journey he simply had to make. He spoke of this compulsion in terms of God's call: 'The Lord ... took me from herding the flock and ... said "Go".' Amos went because he had a strong sense of having been sent. In a similar way, in the gospel reading, the disciples set out on a journey because they are sent on that journey by Jesus. They set out freely, but in response to a call, a sending.

The experience of Amos and the disciples is also very often our experience. The second reading speaks about the mystery of God's purpose. God has a purpose for our lives. That same reading speaks about God's choice. God has chosen us to live in a certain way, chosen us to journey as Christ did. Although we are constantly making all kinds of journeys of our own choosing, there is a more fundamental journey that God has chosen for us. God's choice, God's purpose, impinges on us throughout our lives, prompting us to take certain paths and to avoid others, moving us to set out in one direction rather than another. The shape of the journey that God has chosen for us is visible in the life of Christ. God never ceases to call us to walk in the way of his Son. Although God has chosen this journey for us, God also wants us to choose this journey for ourselves, and God waits for us to do so. This is not a choice we make once and for all. Rather, it is a choice we are constantly remaking. Throughout our lives we keep on choosing to surrender to God's purpose for our lives; we keep on setting out on the journey God is calling us to take.

If we keep on choosing the journey that God has chosen for us, striving to respond to God's call, this will impact on all the various smaller journeys we take in life. It will influence the way we holiday for example. We will choose to holiday in ways that are genuinely recreational, that truly re-create us in the image of God's Son. We will relax in ways that are really life-giving for ourselves and for others, in ways that help us to become more fully the person God has chosen us to be.

The readings this morning invite us to become more attuned to the call of God, so that we journey in the Lord's way. Like Amos and the disciples, we may feel anxious and uncertain before this call but, in heeding that call, we are assured of what the second reading calls 'the richness of the grace that God has showered upon us'. The Lord does not send us out on the journey he has chosen for us without providing for us along the way. As we try to be faithful to the Lord's way, we will experience, in the words of today's Psalm, the Lord's saving help.

Sixteenth Sunday in Ordinary Time

You hear a lot of talk about the importance of planning nowadays. Businesses, schools, state agencies make mention of a two-year plan or a five-year plan or a ten-year plan. We are also aware that as individuals we need to plan. At a certain moment on our life's journey, the need to plan can be felt more strongly. In particular, when we reach something of a crossroads in our lives, we tend to take stock and plan for our future.

In the gospel reading, we find Jesus with a very clear plan for himself and his disciples. The disciples had been away on a missionary journey. The demands of work had been exhausting. The gospel reading says that 'the apostles had no time even to eat'. Jesus planned to take them away to some lonely place all by themselves so that they could rest awhile. Jesus recognised that there was more to life than work. Yes, the harvest is plentiful and the labourers are few. There is always more work to be done. Yet, Jesus would not allow his disciples to be taken over by work or by other people. Stepping back can help to give balance to our lives, can bring home to us that we are more than what we do.

Yet, although Jesus had a plan for himself and his disciples, that plan was frustrated by unexpected circumstances. As he stepped ashore with his disciples to what he thought would be a quiet place, there was a crowd waiting for them. The hoped for deserted place had become a village. So much for the plan and for the value that the plan expressed! Jesus responded, not by getting annoyed, or making a speech about his need for privacy, but by showing compassion for the crowd, and by setting himself to feed their spiritual hunger by teaching them at length. By his action he showed that people were more important than plans, and that plans were ultimately at the service of people and not *vice versa*. Although Jesus' plans were frustrated, what eventually transpired, which was not planned for, was something truly memorable. Having fed the hungry crowd with his word, he went on to feed them with some bread and some fish, which is next Sunday's gospel reading.

We can all point to plans, hopes and aspirations that were important to us, and yet that eventually came to nothing. We can be quite troubled when our plans do not work out. Especially if we have put a lot of time and energy into some plan or other and it does not transpire, we can feel depressed and angry. Yet, today's gospel reading reminds us that the failure of our plans can create a space for something really worthwhile to happen that we had not planned for at all. The failure of our plan can create an unexpected opportunity. When something does not work out as we had planned, it can be good to step back and to ask ourselves: 'What new possibility might now be emerging from the failure of this plan?' What appears initially to be a set back can in the end turn out to be a blessing.

We believe that, above and beyond our own plans and purposes, there is a higher purpose, God's purpose. That purpose of God is driven by his compassion, the compassion Jesus displayed in the gospel reading when he saw the crowds like sheep without a shepherd. The readings today speak about the purpose of God in a variety of ways. According to the first reading, God's purpose is to gather together his scattered people; according to the responsorial psalm, it is to guide us along the right path, to lead us near restful waters; according to the second reading, God's purpose is to break down the barriers that separate us from each other and from God.

God is constantly taking new initiatives to bring that compassionate purpose of his to pass. The death of Jesus on Calvary shows that God can work powerfully to fulfil his purpose even in the most unpromising of situations. Golgotha was not something that the disciples had planned for. We believe that God's purpose for our lives continues to work itself out even when our own purposes and plans come to nothing. Indeed, it appears that God can sometimes work more powerfully in the seeming chaos that can flow from our plans not working out than in the order that would have been created if our plans had worked out. Today's readings invite us to hold our plans lightly, and to trust that even when they fail, God's purpose for our lives prevails. Whether our plans work out or not, God remains the good shepherd who continues to guide us along the right path.

Seventeenth Sunday in Ordinary Time

From time to time we can find ourselves facing into situations that seem beyond our resources to manage. It might be the onset of a serious illness in our own lives or in the lives of those we love. We wonder how we will get through the challenging times that lie ahead. It might be the sudden death of a family member or a close friend. We wonder how we will ever be able to keep going without the person who has meant so much to us. It might be the case that our lives have taken a turning we very much regret. We wonder how we will ever get beyond this lapse and make a fresh start. In all kinds of ways we can find ourselves facing a future that seems uninviting.

In this morning's gospel reading we find Jesus and his disciples facing a situation that seemed beyond their resources to cope with. They were faced with a hungry crowd and little or no means of feeding them. In this situation different people reacted in different ways. Philip made a calculation on the basis of the number of people and the amount of money available to buy food, and decided that nothing could be done. This was the reaction of the realist. Andrew has another reaction to the situation. He recognised that one of the crowd had a small amount of food but he dismissed this small resource as of no value. This is the reaction of the pessimist.

There were two other reactions in the story that the gospel tells. The small boy willing gave to Jesus the few pieces of food that he had. This is the reaction of the generous person, of the one who is prepared to give all he or she has, even though it appears to be far less than what is needed. Such people are wonderful to have around when challenging times come our way. Then there is the reaction of Jesus himself. He took the few resources that the young boy was generous enough to part with and, having prayed the prayer of thanksgiving to God over these small pieces of food, he somehow fed the enormous crowd. As a result, everyone had more than enough to eat and there was even some food left over.

St Paul once made the great discovery that God's power can be made perfect in weakness. In the gospel reading, Jesus works powerfully in and through what were, from a merely human point of view, very weak resources indeed, five barley loaves and two fish. Philip, Andrew, and all the other disciples, discovered that the impossible became possible in the power and prayer of Jesus. The Lord needs our resources of generosity and giftedness today as much as he needed the five barley loaves and the two fish of that young boy, if he is to continue to do his work in the world, if he is to feed those who hunger for food, for love, for God. In responding to all those hungers of his people today, the Lord will not bypass our own resources. They may seem very inadequate to us, but to the Lord they are vital. He asks us to give ourselves and our resources generously to him, to place all that we have and all that we are at his disposal. If we do that, we can never underestimate what the Lord can do in our own lives and in the lives of others through us.

Today's second reading is from the letter to the Ephesians. Immediately before that reading, St Paul declared that God's power 'at work within us is able to accomplish abundantly far more than all we can ask or imagine'. We can be surprised at what the Lord's power can accomplish within us and through us if we give of ourselves generously to him. Often our faith is not expectant enough. We can fail to appreciate how powerfully the risen Lord can work through generous lives.

If we believe in a Lord whose power at work within us can do immeasurably more than all we ask or image, we will always remain people of hope, no matter how hopeless things may seem. Paul reminds us in that second reading that we are all called into one and the same hope. As Christians we are not disposed to writing off any situation, or any person, as hopeless. We never despair before the enormity of the task that lies before us, whether that task relates to our own situation or the situation of those in greater need than ourselves. We continue to give generously of the little we have, even when the mountain ahead seems beyond reach, because we know how powerfully the Lord can work through our generous efforts.

Eighteenth Sunday in Ordinary Time

We all have needs which drive us to seek to have those needs met. At the most basic level, we need food and water in order to live. We have other, less physical, needs, such as the need for intimacy. We all need friends, people we can confide in and share our lives with. We have spiritual needs, the need to reach out to a greater power beyond ourselves that can draw us towards ultimate values, such as truth, freedom and justice.

The first reading is set in the context of the wilderness between Egypt and Canaan. The people of Israel had lived in Egypt, a foreign land, for many generations, where they were slaves of the Pharaoh. Their need and longing for freedom was finally responded to when God called Moses to lead them out of slavery in Egypt towards the Promised Land. Freedom is, indeed, a basic need, both personal freedom and communal freedom. When it is denied, it can give rise to deep resentment and even violent revolt. A person whose needs for food and drink are carefully met, but whose need for freedom is denied, is likely to be deeply unhappy. In today's first reading, however, the people's need for freedom had been responded to, but their more basic need for food and water was not being met. They expressed the view to Moses that slavery in Egypt where they were well fed was preferable to freedom in the wilderness where they were starving. Important human needs can seem of little consequence if still more basic needs are not being met. The Lord responded to his people's cry for food in the wilderness. The scriptures suggest that the Lord works on the principle of first things first. Feeding the hungry, giving drink to the thirsty, clothing the naked, housing the homeless, all come before other forms of ministry.

Today's gospel reading follows on from last Sunday's gospel reading, where Jesus fed the hungry multitude in the wilderness with bread and fish. Jesus unhesitatingly fed the physical hunger of the crowd. Today's gospel reading is set in the context of the day after that feeding. The same crowd approach Jesus looking for more of the same. On this occasion, however, Jesus attempts to move them beyond their preoccupation with physical food to deeper realities. He seeks to lead them beyond too great a focus on their physical needs towards a greater attention to their spiritual needs. 'Do not work for food that cannot last, but work for food that endures to eternal life.' The sense of what Jesus is calling for might better be expressed as: 'Do not only work for food that cannot last, but work also for food that endures to eternal life.' Jesus is calling on them to pay attention to the deeper hungers and thirsts in their lives. That call of Jesus remains very pertinent in this part of the world where most peoples' basic needs for food, clothing and shelter are met, and where the danger is that people will immerse ourselves in the pursuit of the material to the neglect of the spiritual.

Jesus goes on in that gospel reading to present himself as the bread of life, as the one who can satisfy those deeper hungers and thirsts in our hearts. It is in coming to him, believing in him, relating to him, that our hunger for the food that endures to eternal life will be met. Our deepest longings can be satisfied by Jesus the Bread of Life. Our longing for truth, for ultimate meaning, can be met by the one who said of himself: 'I am the truth.' Our longing for a love that is enduring and reliable can be met by the one who displayed a 'greater love' on the cross. Our longing for reassurance that we are forgiven and accepted in spite of past failures can be met by the one who is the Lamb of God who came to take away the sin of the world. Our longing for a life that will never end is met by the one who declared himself to be the resurrection and the life. Our longing to serve others can be met by the one who washed the feet of his disciples and called on them to do for each other what he had done for them.

In the gospel reading, Jesus calls on the crowd to 'work' for the food that endures to eternal life, and then goes on to explain this 'work of God' in terms of believing in the one whom God has sent. Good works are secondary to this one work of believing in Jesus and responding to his call to 'come and see'. In responding to that call, good works of various kinds will indeed follow.

Nineteenth Sunday in Ordinary Time

The story of Elijah in the first reading is one that we might find easy to identify with. Elijah had experienced great hostility to his mission from a very powerful woman in the land, named Jezebel. Her opposition discouraged him to the point where he was almost ready to give up. We are all aware of forces in our own experience that discourage us and take away our enthusiasm to engage with life. These forces can take many forms, such as other people, or some event or circumstance, perhaps some experience of disappointment or failure. The temptation to give up and to pack in what we know in our heart of hearts is worthwhile can be very strong. Elijah took refuge in sleep, and sleep can be a helpful way of coping with a reality that we find too difficult to bear.

Yet, what ultimately enabled Elijah to keep going was not sleep, but what the first reading calls, 'an angel of the Lord'. In the Jewish scriptures, an 'angel' is a messenger from the Lord. This messenger touched Elijah and brought him very simple provisions, a baked scone and a jar of water. These simple resources enabled Elijah to journey on, until he reached his destination. We believe that the Lord continues to send messengers to us in our need. We are all called to be messengers of the Lord to one other. In the second reading, Paul elaborates on this calling we have each received when he writes: 'Be friends with one another, and kind ... follow Christ by loving as he loved you.' The Lord can call on any one of us to provide the equivalent of the baked scone and the jar of water for someone who has lost energy for the journey of life. We are often called to be the Lord's messenger to someone in very simple ways. A listening ear, a thoughtful word, some simple gesture – all can have a power for good that can bring new life to others.

The gospel story of the journey to Emmaus is a story about a messenger from God coming to touch the lives of two people who had lost heart. When Jesus joined the two disciples on the road to Emmaus, he first invited them to tell their story. Having listened to their story, he then spoke a word to them that was shaped by the scriptures. That simple human gesture of walking attentively with the two disciples, listening to them and speaking with them, had a profound impact on them. Jesus shows us in that story what we are all called to be. We are to journey with each other in ways that give fresh heart to one another. We are called to be food and drink for the journey for each other. Whenever others experience us as bread of life then indeed we show ourselves to be messengers of the risen Lord

The Lord who comes to us through his various messengers, comes to us in a special way through the Eucharist that we are now celebrating. If we are called to be bread of life for each other, we believe that we receive the bread of life in the full sense in the Eucharist. In today's gospel reading, Jesus speaks of himself as the bread of life. After the Lord listened to the two disciples on the road to Emmaus and spoke a life-giving word to them, he then led them to the table where they recognised him in the breaking of bread. The risen Lord, who comes to us in life through his messengers, leads us to the table of the Eucharist for a fuller and more complete meeting with him. The Eucharist is a moment to pause on our life's journey and to receive, as Elijah did, the Lord's provisions. Just as the angel said to Elijah: 'Get up and eat', so the Lord says to all of us at the Eucharist: 'Take and eat.'

We bring to the Eucharist everything that we have gathered on our life-journey, our joys and our sorrows, our hopes and our disappointments, our failures and our achievements, and we lay them all before the Lord. The Lord receives our story, our experiences and, in response, he feeds us with what Jesus refers to in the gospel reading as 'my flesh, for the life of the world'. Through the Eucharist he strengthens us for the road ahead. When Elijah took to the road again, strengthened by the food and drink, he set off for the mountain of God, the place of God's presence. The road we travel together as Christians also leads ultimately to the place of God's presence, that heavenly banquet at which the Lord is the generous host, and of which the Eucharist is the anticipation.

Twentieth Sunday in Ordinary Time

It can be tempting to give out about the age in which we live. We can be very aware of the shortcomings of our time and culture. We often complain of falling standards in all walks of life. We are conscious of a breakdown in community, a decline in moral values, a fracturing of family life. The increase in the suicide rate, especially among young men, is disturbing evidence that many people experience our times as devoid of meaning. We could easily get discouraged about our contemporary society.

I was struck by the statement of Paul in today's second reading: 'This may be a wicked age, but your lives should redeem it.' In his letter to the Romans he says something similar: 'Do not be overcome by evil, but overcome evil with good.' Paul was well aware of the dark side of his own culture. Yet, that reality did not discourage him. He was convinced that the lives of believers could redeem the age in which they lived. We don't often think of ourselves as redeemers. We tend to reserve the term 'redeemer' for Christ. Yet, Paul is prepared to extend that term to all those who have been baptised into Christ. He recognises that the Lord working through us can redeem the time, the age, in which we live. We can never underestimate the extent to which the Lord can make us a force for good, a source of life and light, in our world.

As Christians we recognise that if the Lord is to work in a redeeming and life-giving way through us, we need to keep our relationship with him alive. In the first reading, the Wisdom of God calls on people to come to her so as to eat the bread and drink the wine of her teaching. In the gospel reading, Jesus, the true wisdom of God, goes further and calls on his disciples, not only to come to him, but to eat his flesh and drink his blood. This kind of language must have seemed shocking. We can sympathise with the Jews who asked: 'How can this man give us his flesh to eat?' Yet, in spite of the hostile reaction to his words, Jesus did not try to speak in a way that was more acceptable to his hearers. The language of eating his flesh and drinking his blood was not up for negotiation.

The call of Jesus to come to him raises no hackles, but his call: 'Eat me', still has the power to make us sit up a bit. In calling on us to eat his flesh and drink his blood, Jesus shows us just how deeply he wants to be in communion with us. It is the Eucharist that makes possible that depth of communion between us and the Lord that he desires. The Lord wants us not merely to come to him, but to consume him. He wants us to take him into ourselves, to really digest him, in the sense of making our own his outlook on life, his values, his attitudes, his way of relating. In absorbing him in this way he promises that we will come to share in his very life: 'Whoever eats me will draw life from me.' Whenever we eat food, the food becomes part of us; it lives in us. When we receive the Lord in the Eucharist, he does not become part of us. Rather we become part of him; we live with his own life. This is a life that never ends. 'Anyone who eats my flesh and drinks my blood has eternal life.'

The Lord offers us this level of communion with himself so that our own lives may redeem the times in which we live. The life that we receive from the Lord in the Eucharist is to flow through us and ennoble the world of which we are a part. When we say 'Amen' before receiving communion, we are not only saying 'I believe this is the body of Christ', but we are also saying 'Amen' to the Lord dwelling in our lives so that he may carry out his life-giving mission in the world through us.

The Eucharist is at the heart of the church's life. The late Pope John Paul II in his Encyclical Letter on the Eucharist puts it this way: 'The church has received the Eucharist from Christ her Lord not as one gift – however precious – among so many others, but as the gift *par excellence*, for it is the gift of himself in his sacred humanity, as well as the gift of his saving work.' We receive the Lord's gift of himself in this Eucharist so that his saving work can continue in our world through our lives.

Twenty-First Sunday of the Year

Most of us were probably baptised as infants. Our parents presented us for baptism shortly after we were born. They sensed that becoming a Christian was a blessing that they should open us up to at a very early age. At baptism we were united with Christ in a special way, becoming members of his body, the church, receiving a share of his Spirit, who prompted us to cry out 'Abba, Father' to God, as Christ did. In presenting us for baptism, our parents were making a fundamental decision on our behalf. They made that decision because they valued their own relationship with Christ and with his church.

All of us at Mass here this morning are grateful to our parents for making such a decision for us so early in our lives. As we grew into childhood and then into adolescence and into adulthood, we will have had opportunities to make our own the decision our parents made for us. Your presence here at Mass today is a sign that you have done just that. The weekly Eucharist is our opportunity to renew our baptism, to keep on making for ourselves the choice of Christ that our parents made for us. The Eucharist has always been understood in the church since the earliest days as a sacrament of initiation, the third sacrament of initiation after baptism and confirmation. Of the three sacraments of initiation, the Eucharist is the only one that we celebrate repeatedly. We can only be baptised and confirmed once, whereas we can celebrate the Eucharist on a weekly or even a daily basis. Because the Eucharist is a sacrament of initiation, in coming to the Eucharist we are making a statement that we want to belong to Christ and to his church.

There may be times in our lives when we are unsure whether or not we want to go on making that statement. We can find ourselves hesitating, and for a whole variety of reasons. We are given a good example of such hesitation among believers in today's gospel reading. The evangelist tells us that many of Jesus' followers found his teaching on the Eucharist intolerable. They could not accept his talk about the need to eat his flesh and to drink his blood. As a result, the evangelist tells us, 'many of his disciples left him and stopped going with him'. Even in Jesus' own lifetime, not everyone who became one of his disciples went on to remain one. Jesus did not hold on to people against their will. In the gospel reading he even turns to the twelve and says to them: 'What about you, do you want to go away too?' Even though he had chosen them for a special mission, he waited on them to choose him freely, without compulsion. Jesus' teaching on the Eucharist was a moment of decision for his disciples. It brought to a head where they stood – did they want to stay with him or leave him? Did they want to confirm their initial decision to be his followers or to reverse it?

The Eucharist remains that kind of moment of decision today for Jesus' disciples. Our presence or absence at the Eucharist can be making an important statement about where we stand in regard to Christ and his church. Even though there may be people here this morning who wonder about the strength of their faith and who are very aware of the reality of religious doubt within themselves, your presence here is a sign that at some level you want to make your own Peter's confession of faith in today's gospel reading: 'Lord who shall we go to? You have the message of eternal life, and we believe; we know that you are the Holy One of God.'

Many of those who were baptised into Christ have ceased to come to Sunday Eucharist, as we know. Yet, many of these do come to Mass at Christmas and Easter. That too is a statement. They have not given up on the Eucharist completely or on Christ and his church, and he has certainly not given up on them. The Lord continues to draw us to himself, even when, like the disciples in the gospel reading, we stop going with him. In drawing us, he awaits our assent to being drawn. Our assent to the drawing of the Lord can take time to mature and it can involve many twists and turns. Peter, who made the wonderful confession of faith in today's gospel reading, went on to deny the Lord publicly. Yet, the Lord gave Peter the opportunity to renew his earlier public profession of faith. The Lord gives us the same opportunity and he will give it as often as we need it.

Twenty Second Sunday of the Year

Our families of origin tend to have their own traditions. In being born into a particular family, we inherit traditional ways of doing things that have been part of the story of our family. When a family member breaks with those traditions, it can often create some initial tension in the family. Yet, every generation within a family has to creatively shape the family tradition in ways that correspond to the culture and times in which they live. Tradition is not a kind of dead weight to be passed on faithfully from one generation to the next. Any tradition that is worthwhile has to be living and vibrant, capable of change and development. A living tradition is one that embodies the wisdom of the past while being open to new wisdom that comes from further reflection on experience.

If every family has its tradition, this is even more so of the church which is two thousand years old. Within the Roman Catholic Church in particular, tradition has always been recognised as a source of God's revelation. God speaks to us through the scriptures, but also through all of those people who from the earliest days of the church have reflected upon and given expression to the scriptures in their way of life. The church's tradition is a living tradition. Like a human body it grows and develops. There is always continuity with the past but also change and new life. Looking back over the history of the church, it is possible to identify moments when the church's tradition underwent a very significant development. The Second Vatican Council in the early 1960s was one such a moment, when the whole church made a serious effort to listen to the signs of the times and to allow the church's tradition to be reshaped accordingly.

Jesus was born into a Jewish family and inherited the traditions of his Jewish faith. The gospels suggest that he understood himself as sent by God to launch a kind of Second Vatican Council within Judaism. He respected deeply the Jewish tradition he inherited but he wanted to reshape it so that it came to express more fully God's purpose for the Jewish people and for all of humanity. This mission to renew and reshape the Jewish tradition brought him into conflict with those who wanted to maintain the tradition as it was. A good example of such conflict is to be found in our gospel reading this morning. The Pharisees who were committed to preserving and promoting the traditions of the elders accused Jesus and his disciples of riding roughshod over these traditions. Jesus in turn declared that the Pharisees give more importance to human traditions than to God's commandments. While very concerned about traditions relating to food – what is eaten and how it is eaten – they had neglected much more fundamental values in God's eyes, what Jesus refers to elsewhere as the weightier matters of the law, such as mercy, justice and love. Jesus challenged the upholders of the tradition to pay less attention to externals and to attend more to what is within the human heart and to the actions that flow from that. He was calling on them to get back to basics, to return to the wellsprings of their tradition, as found in the prophet Isaiah, whom Jesus quotes.

The Second Vatican Council was the church's attempt to get back to basics. What drove the deliberations of the Council was a desire to return to the sources of our faith – to scripture and to the earliest traditions of the church. Every religious tradition needs ongoing purification and the path to that purification always involves a return to the sources. Today's readings invite us as a church and as individuals to keep on returning to the sources of our faith, in particular, the scriptures, the word of God. In the second reading, St James calls on us to 'accept and submit to the word which has been planted in you'. Such submission to God's word, he goes on to say, involves not just listening to that word but doing what the word tells us. For James, central to God's word is the call to show care and concern for the needy and most vulnerable. In returning to the sources of our faith, we will always hear afresh the call to serve each other and to build each other up. It is clear from today's gospel reading that Jesus was much more concerned about how people were relating to each other than about food regulations. Today's readings remind us that for us as Christians, the real traditionalists, those most faithful to our Christian tradition, are people who live in ways that give expression to the healing, compassionate and life-giving presence of the Lord.

Twenty-Third Sunday of the Year

We can all think of people who have enriched our lives in one way or another, friends and family who have helped to bring out the best in us, who have helped us to become all that God is calling us to be. We cannot really be all that God wants us to be without the support and the help of others. There is so much we can receive only in relationship with others.

In the gospel reading this morning a deaf and dumb man is brought to Jesus by others. There were obviously people in this man's community who were looking out for him, and they brought him to someone they believed could be of help to him. They led him to a person that he could not have reached by himself. They were a live-giving presence in his life. That kind of scene is repeated more than once in the gospels. Another example is that passage where a paralysed man was brought into the presence of Jesus by a group of his friends, even though it meant that they had to create a hole in the roof of the house where Jesus was staying.

Such gospel scenes are repeated in the lives of people today. People who help to bring the sick to places like Lourdes become the hands and legs, the eyes and ears of those who are seriously disabled. There are many who do this work without travelling to Lourdes or elsewhere. Within the confines of their own home or neighbourhood, they are a life-giving presence for others, and are present to them in ways that enable them to live fuller lives. We all have that capacity to make life richer for others. God's creative and life-giving spirit is latent in all of us. To the extent that we are in touch with that creative spirit of God within, wonderful things can happen through us and the lives of others can be greatly enriched.

There was a film some years ago called *The Secret Garden*. The main character was a young boy called Colin. He was a sickly child who had been overprotected because of his illness, and had never learned to communicate his feelings. It was his lively friends who helped him find the secret garden, a garden in the grounds of an old house. It was in that garden, to which he had been led by his friends, that Colin found a lost part of himself. Factors external to him had impeded Colin's growth, but his friends helped him to discover who he really was and enabled him make contact with his deepest self. As a result, he came alive in new ways. His friends had become for him channels of the creative spirit of God.

The gospel reading this morning reminds us that we need others to help us become the person God desires us to be. We need compassionate and concerned people to take us to those secret gardens that have life-giving power, and that would remain a secret to us if others didn't show them to us. In various ways any one of us can become a gate to life-giving gardens for others. The God in whom we believe is a Creator God. We are all called to be channels of God's ongoing creative work. God desires to work through us in creative ways so that the lives of others are enriched. We can all help each other to attain what Paul in one of his letters refers to as the glorious freedom of the children of God.

In today's gospel reading the man who people brought to Jesus was both deaf and had an impediment in his speech. It was only when his ears were opened by Jesus that he began to speak clearly. The healing of his deafness was prior to the healing of his speech impediment. This is a reminder to us that our ability to speak is dependent on our capacity to listen. Listening comes before speaking. This is also true in our dealings with others. Our capacity to hear others, to really listen to them, can be more important that anything we might say to them, or do for them. One of the ways we mediate God's creative power to others is listening attentively to them. That act of listening can be powerfully life-giving in its own right, even before we say or do anything on their behalf. When people are listened to in a non-judgemental way, they can begin to come alive in new ways.

In the light of today' readings, we might pray this Sunday for the grace to discern the ways in which the Lord may be calling each of us to be channels of his creative power in our world today.

Twenty-Fourth Sunday in Ordinary Time

We are familiar with the saying: 'Actions speak louder than words.' What people do is more revealing of who they are than what they say. If people say one thing and do another, it is what they do that ultimately shapes our perception of them. St James in the second reading expresses his conviction that our relationship with God is revealed much more by how we behave than by what we say. He is rather dismissive of those who say 'I have faith' and yet, as he puts it, have 'never done a single good act'.

Jesus would not have disagreed with James in this regard. He once spoke a parable in which the son, who told his father that he would not go into the vineyard to work, but subsequently changed his mind and went, is to be preferred to the son who told his father that he would go into the vineyard, but subsequently did not do so. When it comes to our relationship with the Lord, actions do speak louder than words.

Yet, today's gospel reading suggests that for Jesus words and what we mean by them are important in assessing the quality of our relationship with God. When Jesus asked his disciples 'Who do you say that I am?' Peter spoke up on behalf of them all and declared: 'You are the Messiah.' At one level, these words of Peter were perfectly acceptable. Jesus was the long-awaited Jewish Messiah. Yet, at another level, what Peter meant by these words, how Peter was thinking, was completely at odds with how Jesus was thinking. When Jesus went on to reveal that as Messiah he would also be the suffering and rejected Son of Man, Peter rebuked him. This was not the kind of Messiah Peter had in mind. He clearly did not see himself as the follower of a crucified Messiah. Peter's rebuke of Jesus earned Peter an even stronger rebuke from Jesus: 'Get behind me, Satan! Because the way you think is not God's way but man's.' Jesus was very critical of Peter's mindset – a mindset that was revealed in what Peter said and would subsequently reveal itself in what Peter and the other disciples did, when they took flight at the time of Jesus' passion.

Today's gospel reading suggests that Jesus was very interested in the mindset that was at the root of how people both spoke and acted. He wanted his followers to have God's mindset on things,

God's perspective. That is why Jesus invested a lot of time and energy in teaching his disciples. In his teaching he was trying to communicate his own mindset and perspective to his disciples, so that his mindset would become theirs as well. In today's gospel reading Jesus teaches that remaining true to God's calling and getting involved in God's work will often mean travelling the way of the cross. He was teaching his followers that they must be ready to choose that way if remaining faithful to God's values requires it. Faced with such teaching, Jesus' disciples showed themselves to be reluctant learners.

If today's second reading declares that how we act is more significant than how we speak, in revealing our relationship with God, the gospel reading suggests that more important than both is how we think. Our way of thinking about God, our understanding of God, will invariably influence what we say and what we do. A distorted understanding of God can do great damage, as we know.

Thinking correctly about God has always been a value within Christianity from the beginning. We are encouraged to bring our minds to bear on who God is, who Jesus is, on what it means to be a follower of Jesus. Our faith must always be a faith that seeks understanding. When it comes to God and God's Son all of us remain learners, including those who have the ministry of teaching within the church. This kind of learning is not just a human endeavour; it has to be a graced endeavour. We need the light of the Holy Spirit if we are to think in God's way and, out of that, speak and act in God's way.

In today's gospel reading, Jesus calls on Peter and the other disciples to change their way of thinking. That change Jesus called for was a long time in coming, according to Mark's gospel. Jesus' efforts to teach his disciples continued to meet with resistance. Yet, he persevered with them. We too can be slow learners when it comes to the things of God. Yet, the Lord perseveres with us; he remains our teacher; he continues to give us the Spirit of Truth who will lead us into the complete truth. What he looks for from us is openness to being led.

Twenty-Fifth Sunday in Ordinary Time

Arguments and disagreements are part and parcel of life. Different people can see the same issue very differently, and each person will always be ready to argue in favour of their point of view. There are some issues that are worth arguing over until we get as much clarity as possible. There are other issues that are not worth arguing about. We can easily find ourselves getting into unnecessary arguments that serve very little useful purpose.

No doubt, Jesus considered that the argument the disciples were having in today's gospel reading was not one that was serving any great purpose. They were arguing about which of them should be considered the greatest. Unlike Jesus who was ambitious for the coming of God's kingdom, his disciples were ambitious for their own little kingdom. This is the kind of flawed ambition that James talks about in today's second reading, the ambition to get one's own way. This type of ambition, James says, results in wars and battles that can be destructive of others, the kind of battle that the disciples were engaged in at Capernaum.

Of all of the evangelists, Mark is the one who presents the disciples of Jesus in the most negative light. One of the reasons he did that may have been to hold them up as a kind of a mirror to those who would be hearing his gospel. He wanted his hearers to recognise something of themselves in Jesus' first disciples and to hear Jesus' words to his disciples as addressed also to them. The kind of competitiveness that the disciples display in the gospel reading is still very much alive and well today. The mindset of the disciples was that there could only be one winner and for any one of them to win everyone else had to loose; the race was on between them to be that winner. In many ways, this is quite a contemporary mindset that we are all prone to, and yet it is a mindset that is very far removed from that of Jesus whom we claim to follow.

In response to the human tendency to seek greatness for oneself, often at the expense of others, Jesus in today's gospel reading puts before his disciples and before all of us the value of recognising and welcoming greatness in others. There is a world of difference between seeking greatness for oneself and welcoming greatness in others, between seeking honour for oneself and giving honour to others, between a life that is self-serving and one that is at the service of others.

Jesus was aware that true greatness can often be found where it is least expected. To make this point to his argumentative disciples, he took a little child into their midst. In the culture of Jesus' time, the child was considered of little consequence, a symbol of powerlessness, weakness and vulnerability, totally lacking in honour and prestige. Yet, Jesus goes on to identify himself fully with the child, and indeed to identify the child with God his Father: 'Whoever welcomes one of these little children in my name, welcomes me; and anyone who welcome me, welcomes … the one who sent me.' Jesus was saying to his disciples: 'This child whom you consider to be of no significance represents me and the one who sent me. What you think of as greatness is worth nothing in God's eyes, what you think as of no value is great in God's eyes.'

Jesus is reminding us that he himself and the God who sent him come to us in the most ordinary and simple of guises. Our primary ambition as the Lord's followers should be to recognise and to welcome the Lord in others, especially in the weakness and vulnerability of others. Our calling is to honour others as we would honour the Lord, to relate to all people as we would relate to the Lord, because the Lord comes to us through those who cross our path, especially through those who would not be considered great by the standards of this world. If our ambition is to recognise and welcome the greatness of others, the Lord in others, then the kind of ambition that prevails among the disciples will not take hold of us.

There is at least one other person in the gospels who exemplifies the kind of ambition that Jesus was trying to promote and that is John the Baptist. Even though Jesus came to him for baptism, John recognised and welcomed the greatness of Jesus, declaring: 'He (Jesus) must increase, but I must decrease.' That is a good motto for all of us who are trying to follow the Lord. We are to live in such a way that the honour always goes to the Lord and not to ourselves.

Twenty-Sixth Sunday in Ordinary Time

More than once I have had the experience of walking along and then suddenly falling forward, having stubbed my foot against a slightly raised paving slab. No doubt, I should be watching more carefully where I am going. Yet sometimes the very paving slabs that are meant to help us walk safely can prove to be a stumbling block because they are out of alignment.

Part of our calling as followers of Jesus is to support each other in that following. We need each other's example, encouragement and, sometimes, challenge if we are to walk in the way of the Lord. Many of us will be able to think of people who inspired us to keep faithful to our baptismal calling. The saints have traditionally played that role in the history of the church. We look to them to show what it means to be the Lord's disciple; they can continue to speak to us across the centuries. We can point to people who are much closer to us in time and place who have done the same for us. They showed us the Lord's way by living that way themselves. Yet, we are also aware that some people can lead us astray, inviting us to take paths that are not in keeping with our baptismal calling. They can become obstacles to us, tripping us up as we struggle to follow Christ's way.

In today's gospel reading, Jesus shows a strong awareness of these two possibilities. He contrasts the one who gives a cup of cold water to one of his followers with the one who is an obstacle to bring down one of his followers. Jesus himself had experienced Peter, the leader of the twelve, as an obstacle to himself. When Peter sought to dissuade Jesus from taking the path that God was asking him to take, because it would involve the cross, Jesus rebuked him with the words: 'You are a stumbling block to me.' (Mt 16:23) Peter was blocking Jesus from doing God's will. In today's gospel reading, we find Jesus' disciples trying to block someone from doing the Lord's work, just because he was not one of the disciples who regularly travelled around with Jesus. In response, Jesus had to rebuke them: 'Do not stop him ... Anyone who is not against us is for us.'

Peter and the disciples meant well in all these cases. We can find ourselves in the role of the stumbling block without realising it. Thinking that our way is the best way, we can then proceed to try and impose that way on others. We too easily identify our way with the Lord's way. The disciples in today's gospel reading had to learn that their way was, in fact, a much narrower way than the Lord's way. Those they judged to be 'not one of us', Jesus judged to be 'for us'. Jesus was able to recognise and encourage goodness wherever he found it. He knew that the Spirit blows where it wills. He was alert to the signs of the Spirit's presence wherever he found them and his response was always one of encouragement and support. In the same way, Moses in the first reading recognised and rejoiced in the movement of the Spirit in the lives of Eldad and Medad.

We each have a role to play in recognising and supporting the working of the Spirit in each other. In writing to the church of Thessalonica Paul says towards the end of his first letter, 'Do not quench the Spirit.' To quench the Holy Spirit in others is to become a stumbling block, an obstacle, to God's working in their lives. We can quench the Spirit, hindering the good work that God is doing in and through others, for a whole variety of very human reasons. We can be motivated by jealousy, as Moses pointedly suggested to the young man who came to him in today's first reading. Like the disciples, we can refuse to acknowledge God's good work in the lives of others because they are not 'one of us', belonging as they do to a different church, a different religion or a different ethnic group. We can be dismissive of the good someone else is doing simply because it is not the way we would have done it, forgetting that the Holy Spirit works in many diverse ways in people's lives. As Paul tells the Corinthians: 'There are varieties of gifts but the same Spirit.' Living as we do in a culture that is awash with obstacles and stumbling blocks to God's working in our lives, we need to ensure that we do not become stumbling blocks for others. The Lord looks to us to give the cup of cold water, to nurture what is good in others.

Twenty-Seventh Sunday in Ordinary Time

Tension is an integral part of most people's lives. Some forms of tension can be quite damaging and can do us harm if we are exposed to it over a long period of time. The kind of tension that is due to prolonged over work comes to mind. Other forms of tension can be quite healthy and necessary, such as the tension generated in us by our efforts to live up to certain ideals and values. We could eliminate this form of tension by watering down our ideals and settling for less. Yet, in our heart of hearts we know that in doing this we are selling ourselves short.

As followers of Christ, our values and ideals are shaped by the message of Jesus in the gospels. The gospel message is demanding as well as consoling. Jesus calls on us to be as generous, as compassionate, as loving as he himself is, as God is. Jesus does not leave us to our own resources in the living out of his values. He gives us the gift of his Holy Spirit whose power at work within us can do immeasurably more than all we ask or imagine. Even with this gift at our disposal, we are all too well aware of our failure to live the life that Jesus calls us to. We know only too well the gap in our lives between the person we are called to be and the person we are. This does create a certain tension in us, but it is the tension associated with being fully alive.

In today's gospel reading, Jesus presents his ideal, God's ideal, for marriage. His teaching went against the grain in the Jewish world of his time. The Jewish law made provision for divorce. The only issue of debate among the religious leaders was the grounds for divorce. One school of rabbis favoured very lenient grounds; another school insisted on much stricter grounds. According to the Jewish law it was only the man who could initiate divorce proceedings, whatever the grounds. The woman was not free to do the same. The divorce laws gave a freedom to men that it did not give to women, and it left women very vulnerable to being cut adrift by their husbands. In that context, Jesus' teaching was intended to protect women. It reminded men of their obligation to love their wives as they would their own body, rather than seeing her almost as a piece of property that they could dispose of when it suited them. Jesus went back to God's original intention as expressed in the Book of Genesis, according to which husband and wife are to become one body, one loving union.

There is a wonderful vision of marriage here. St Paul developed it when he stated that the union between a husband and wife is a reflection of the union between Christ and his church and that husbands are to love their wives, and wives their husbands, as Christ loves the church. Those who come to the church to be married are drawn by this vision of Jesus for marriage. It is not by accident that one of the most frequently chosen readings for the wedding liturgy is that of Paul's great hymn to love in 1 Corinthians 13: 'Love is patient, love is kind ...' Here indeed is Jesus' ideal for married love, the spelling out of what it means to live as one body. Yet, we are all aware that the gap between that ideal and the real can be very great, in marriage as much as in other areas of life. Marriages do break down, sometimes irretrievably so. Jesus must have been very aware of this. His attitude towards those who were not living according to his ideal for marriage was always characterised by sensitivity and respect. The way the gospels show him relating to the Samaritan woman and to the women caught in the act of adultery shows this.

Jesus, it seems, could present the ideal clearly and at the same time make allowances for the reality of people's lives which often fell far short of the ideal. There is a message here for all of us, not just in relation to marriage but in relation to other areas of life. We need ideals and values that will put before us a way that does justice to what is best in us. We will find such ideals and values in the message and life of Jesus. However, we also need an assurance that when we fail to live out these values, for whatever reason, we remain graced people who are loved by God and continue to be called into communion with God's Son. We will find such an assurance too in the message and life of Jesus.

Twenty-Eighth Sunday in Ordinary Time

One of the tasks of life for all of us is getting our priorities right. As we go through life we try to clarify for ourselves what is worth valuing and what is not. In the course of a lifetime we may discover that what we once valued is not so important after all, and we may also discover that what we once dismissed as of no value is truly important.

Our desires, our longings, reveal what it is we truly value. Because our longings often find expression in our prayers, if we are people of faith, very often what we pray for reveals what we value most. In today's first reading we are given the prayer of King Solomon. Here was a man who, because of his position, could have had as many possessions as he wanted. Yet, according to our reading, what he valued more than riches was wisdom, and it was for this that he prayed. As leader of a nation, he understood that wisdom was what he needed more than anything else, and he also recognised that wisdom was ultimately a gift that came from God.

If our prayers reveal our values, so too at times can our questions. In today's gospel reading, a man runs up to Jesus and asks him a question: 'Good master, what must I do to inherit eternal life?' The content of his questions reveals what was of greatest value to him – the gaining of eternal life. Yet, there turns out to be a tragic quality to this man. Having asked his question, he was unable to live with the answer that Jesus gave: 'Go and sell everything you own and give the money to the poor ... then come, follow me.'

What Jesus asked of this particular man, he did not ask of everyone who approached him. He called different people in different ways. To a man whom he had released from his demons he said: 'Go home to your friends, and tell them how much the Lord has done for you.' To the leper he cured Jesus said: 'Get up and go on your way.' The Lord called people in ways that were appropriate to their situation.

In the case of the man in our gospel reading, Jesus prefaced his call to him by stating: 'There is one thing you lack.' This particular man lacked a certain detachment. He was overly dependant on his possessions. Jesus' call challenged him where he most needed to be challenged, if his deep longing for eternal life was to be satisfied. Having heard the call, the man went away sad. Jesus' word to him was alive and active, as today's second reading declares. It cut into him like a double-edged sword, seeking to separate him from his excessive attachment to his wealth. In response, the man backed away from Jesus' word. Having run excitedly to Jesus, he walked away in sadness.

There are various forms of sadness. There is the sadness that comes from having to let go of our loved ones in death. This comes to all of us sooner or later. With time we can come to some form of acceptance of our loss, and the sadness lifts. There is also the sadness of the man in the gospel reading today. This is the sadness that comes over us when we fail to follow through on our values, when we do not take the path that in our heart of hearts we want to take, when we live in ways that sell us short and are not in keeping with how we want to live.

What Jesus said to the man in the gospel reading, 'One thing you lack', he might be saying to any one of us. There can be a lack in us that blocks us from taking the path that is true to what is best in us and prevents us from responding to the Lord's call. What the man in the gospel reading lacked was the freedom to let go of his great wealth. Our particular lack may be quite different. We can have all kinds of attachments that hold us back from taking the path the Lord is calling us to take. Like the rich man, there may be something we need to do in order to take the path that leads to life, but we sense a great reluctance in us to do it.

In doing what we need to do we are not left to our own resources. The Lord is there to help us and Jesus assures us that 'everything is possible for God'. Like Solomon in today's first reading, we are invited to turn to God in prayer and to ask for whatever help we need to take the path of life.

Twenty-Ninth Sunday in Ordinary Time

Most of us have had the experience of asking for something and not getting it. That experience begins in childhood when we begin to learn the difficult lesson that others do not automatically respond to our wants and whims. In adolescence we discover that our peers are not mirror images of ourselves and do not always behave or respond to us in the way we want them to. In adulthood we learn the delicate art of compromise when what we want and what others want come into conflict with each other. We also discover that in our relationship with God our prayers are not always answered, even when they focus not on ourselves but on others and their well-being. The experience of unanswered prayer can be a real challenge to our faith.

In today's gospel reading, James and John come before Jesus with a prayer of petition. They ask him: 'Allow us to sit one at your right hand and the other at your left in your glory.' The previous time Mark had depicted James and John together was on the mount of transfiguration with Peter. There they had an experience of Jesus in his glory, flanked by Moses and Elijah. James and John understood this experience as an anticipation of what was to come, and in the future they wanted the places occupied by Moses and Elijah. Mark emphasises the inappropriateness of this request of James and John by placing it immediately after the third announcement by Jesus of his coming passion and death: 'The Son of Man will be handed over to the chief priests and the scribes, and they will condemn him to death; then they will hand him over to the Gentiles ...' (Mk 10:33-34) As Jesus declares that he is shortly to be humbled, James and John ask Jesus that they be exalted. Here is a prayer that has far too much of 'self' in it. It is not a prayer that Jesus can respond to.

Sometimes, our own prayers can have a lot of 'self' in them, even when they are prayers for others. One dimension of our growing up into the person of Jesus is learning to pray as he prays, entering into his ongoing prayer to the Father. It is only the Holy Spirit who can enable our prayer to harmonise with that of the risen Lord. As Paul states in his letter to the Galatians: 'God has sent the Spirit of his Son into our hearts, crying "Abba"

Father!' (Gal 4:6) In his letter to the Romans he comments that 'The Spirit helps us in our weakness; for we do not know how to pray as we ought, but that very Spirit intercedes with sighs too deep for words.' (Rom 8:26) Our prayer will be a sharing in Jesus' own prayer when it is shaped by the inarticulate sighs of the Spirit deep within us.

In response to the brothers' request of Jesus, he makes his own request of them: 'Can you drink the cup that I must drink, or be baptised with the baptism with which I must be baptised?' Jesus is presented in the gospels as asking many questions. One access point to the gospel story of Jesus for us today is to sit with the many questions that Jesus asks. A very different form of prayer to the prayer of petition is to listen to the various petitions that Jesus addresses to us and, having listened, to respond honestly from the depths of our heart. Jesus' petition to James and John finds an echo in Jesus' own prayer of petition in the garden of Gethsemane: 'Abba, Father, for you all things are possible; remove this cup from me; yet, not what I want, but what you want.' (Mk 14:36) The very cup that Jesus asked James and John to drink, he hesitated to drink himself. Yet, he went on to drink it because his prayer, 'Remove this cup from me', was secondary to his more fundamental prayer, 'Not what I want, but what you want.' Jesus does not request of his disciples anything he is not prepared to do himself. As today's second reading remarks, we have a high priest 'who has been tempted in every way that we are, though he is without sin'. Jesus' petition to James and John is addressed to all of us. He asks if we are prepared to commit ourselves to his servant way, even when it means the way of the cross, the way of self-denial and self-giving. The attentive listener may be put in mind of the sacraments of Eucharist and baptism by Jesus' reference to 'the cup' and 'baptism'. At baptism we are baptised into Jesus' servant way and when we celebrate the Eucharist we renew our commitment to that way.

Thirtieth Sunday in Ordinary Time

Recently, I noticed someone with a blindfold over her eyes and a white stick in her hand. She was attempting to walk without being able to see. She was being guided and helped in this by one or two other people. Because she had a blindfold over here eyes, I understood that she was not in fact blind. However, she was entering into the experience of blindness, presumably for some kind of training purposes. Yet, the awareness that our blindfold can be removed at any time limits the extent to which we can really experience what it is to be blind.

Near the end of the Second World War, an American called John Howard Griffin began to loose his sight while he was still in his twenties. He was told that his loss of sight would eventually be total. He wrote at that time: 'The sight of a pin, a hair, a leaf, a glass of water, the faces of strangers, these filled me with tremendous excitement. I took them in and bound them up in me.' Eventually he became totally blind. In spite of this, he wrote novels, became proficient at music and became a Christian. For twelve years he lived in a world of total darkness. Then in 1957 he miraculously began to see again. A twelve year blockage of the circulation of blood to the optic nerve suddenly opened, restoring his sight. His life became one of rejoicing in the sight he had received back. He threw himself into the civil rights movement until he died in 1980.

John Howard Griffin shared with Bartimaeus in today's gospel reading the wonderful experience of having sight that had been lost restored again. When Jesus asked Bartimaeus: 'What do you want me to do for you?' Bartimaeus' response, 'Master, let me see again', suggests that there was once a time when he could see. Most of us will never know what it means to lose the gift of sight. Like any gift that never leaves us, it is easy to take it for granted. Rejoicing in the gift of sight comes spontaneously to those who have regained this gift having once lost it. Yet, we who have never lost this gift have as much reason for rejoicing in it.

When Jesus asked Bartimaeus: 'What do you want me to do for you?' there was only one answer he could have given: 'Master, let me see again.' When Jesus addresses that same question to us, there are many answers we might feel inclined to give. Perhaps, in line with Bartimaeus' answer, one answer we could give is: 'Lord, help me to use well the gift of sight you have given me.' There are different ways of seeing. Not everything we chose to look upon serves us well or serves others well. We also know from experience that our way of seeing can be quite limiting. A good example of that limited way of seeing is to be found in today's gospel reading. When Bartimaeus first tried to capture Jesus' attention by crying out, 'Son of David, have pity on me', many people rebuked him and told him to keep quiet. They saw this man as a nuisance. Fortunately, Bartimaeus ignored the people who told him to keep quiet and he shouted all the louder, and in doing so he got a very different response from Jesus: 'Call him here.' The very people who saw Bartimaeus as a nuisance were sent by Jesus to Bartimaeus to call him over. They were being invited to see Bartimaeus as Jesus saw him, not as a nuisance, but as a human being in need of help. Jesus' way of seeing this man led to his being healed of his blindness.

The gospel reading today invites us to ask ourselves: 'How do we see others?' 'Do we see them as the Lord sees them?' The people we are tempted to see as nuisances may be those whom the Lord is calling us to serve. Bartimaeus shouted loudly, according to the gospel reading, and people who shout can easily be seen by others as nuisances. Yet, when it comes to personal well-being and the well-being of others, shouting can be in order. Jesus had the capacity to look beyond the shouting of Bartimaeus to the heart of the man out of which the shouting came. This is the kind of seeing that we are all called to, a seeing that sees deeply, that looks beyond what might be an off-putting exterior to the struggle that is going on within the person. This kind of compassionate seeing has its own healing power. When we see as the Lord sees we become channels of his own healing and life-giving presence to others. That is an important dimension of our baptismal calling.

Thirty-First Sunday in Ordinary Time

It is easy to speak in generalities, as we know. It can be tempting to make statements about whole groups of people. Yet, the individual person can always surprise us. Individuals do not always show themselves to be typical of their group. Indeed, each individual human being is an extraordinary mystery.

In the gospels, the scribes as a group tended to be hostile to Jesus. They were experts in the Jewish law and they resented what they saw to be Jesus' unconventional interpretation of the Jewish law. The gospels mention the scribes as one of the groups that were responsible for handing Jesus over to Pilate to be crucified. Yet, not every scribe was a carbon copy of that grouping.

In today's gospel we find a Jewish scribe in respectful dialogue with Jesus. The scribe asked Jesus a serious question. He wanted Jesus to give an opinion as to which of all the 600 plus commandments of the Jewish law was the most important one. Jesus gave him a straight answer: 'This is the first.' Jesus, in fact, gave the scribe more than he asked for. The scribe asked for the first of all the commandments; Jesus gave him the first and the second. The scribe's response to Jesus' answer shows his appreciation: 'Well spoken, Master.' Jesus' subsequent response to the scribe shows how much Jesus appreciated this earnest man: 'You are not far from the kingdom of God.' Here we have two men, who would have been expected to be opponents, showing that they each appreciated the good in the other.

Learning to recognise the good in the other is part of the meaning of what Jesus calls the second commandment: 'Love your neighbour as yourself.' The way that commandment is expressed suggests very strongly that we can only recognise the good in others if we have first recognised the good in ourselves. God's creation is essentially good, and that is especially true of the pinnacle of God's creative work, the human person. We are all too well aware that we are far from being saints. We have regrets around what we have done and what we have failed to do. Yet, for all of that, there is a core of goodness in each one of us, because we have been created by God who alone is all good. The challenge is to recognise and to honour that core of goodness in ourselves and in others, sometimes in spite of the evidence to the contrary. More than any human being, Jesus had that ability to celebrate the goodness of others. Time and time again, the gospels show him recognising and proclaiming the goodness of people who had been written off and labelled as people of no significance. He was, in that sense, the tremendous lover, to quote the title of a book about Jesus that was very popular many years ago. Jesus recognised the good in people and taught others to do the same. On one occasion, he took a child in his arms and declared that whoever receives one such child receives him and whoever receives him receives God who sent him.

Jesus recognised God in others because he knew God, not just with his mind, but with his heart. His knowledge of God was the knowledge born of love. Because Jesus loved God with all his heart, soul, mind and strength, he could recognise God in places and in people where God was not normally noticed. It was Jesus' relationship with God which enabled him to recognize goodness, even when it was hidden from most other people. In the same way, it is our relationship with God, our love of God, our putting God first, that will make it possible for us to recognise God in others, to celebrate the goodness of others, to love others. That is why Jesus declares that the first commandment of all is to love God with all our heart, soul, mind and strength. The most important relationship in our lives to get right is our relationship with God, Jesus is saying. It is only in loving God with our whole being, in giving to God what belongs to God, that we will be able to recognise God in ourselves and in others, and on the basis of that to love and honour ourselves and others.

Because as Christians we believe that Jesus is God with us, for us to love God with our whole being is to love Jesus with our whole being. That is the first commandment. In that sense, it is not surprising that before the risen Lord sent out Peter to shepherd God's people, to love God's people, he first asked him: 'Do you love me?' That is also the Lord's question to all of us.

Thirty-Second Sunday in Ordinary Time

We know from our own experience that the value of a gift does not depend on the amount of money that was spent to buy it. People can put a lot of thought into a gift that costs very little. Others can somewhat thoughtlessly spend a lot of money on a gift. We tend to value more the gift into which a lot of thought has gone than the gift that was expensive. When the gift contains something of the person giving it, we appreciate its worth.

In the gospel reading, Jesus observes two kinds of gifts being given to the temple treasury. Some put a great deal of money into the treasury. Yet, it was the widow's gift of two small pennies that caught Jesus' eye. Even though her small gift was worth little, one sixty-fourth of a day's wages to be exact, it was the most valuable gift of all, because in giving that small sum, she gave her livelihood – she gave her life. Jesus very deliberately points her out to his disciples; he called them over and addressed them in strong tones: 'I tell you solemnly ...' He points to the extraordinary generosity of the widow as someone who has a lot to teach them. Jesus was within a few weeks of his death, when he would be called upon to give everything he had, his whole life. Perhaps he saw in this widow an image of what was soon to be asked of him. He clearly saw her as the kind of inspirational figure his disciples could learn a great deal from.

It is very likely that if Jesus had not pointed out this widow to his disciples, they would not have paid any attention to her. Unlike the scribes who made it their business to be as visible as possible, and about whom Jesus is very critical in today's gospel, this widow was one of the invisible people of the time. The passage reminds us that it is often the people who are least noticed who have the most to teach us. The quality of their goodness and generosity is never on public display. We live among such people without always knowing it. The gospel reading suggests that the quality of goodness and generosity that is invisible to us is always visible to the Lord. He notices even if we do not.

The widow, in putting her two small coins into the temple treasury, believed that she was giving to God. It was to God that she wanted to give her whole livelihood, her life. In a sense, she shows what it means to live the first and the greatest commandment. She loved God with all her heart, soul, mind and strength. Jesus recognised that. God was the focal point of her giving. The gospel reading suggests that for those who gave large sums of money to the temple treasure, the focal point of their giving was much more themselves. Their giving was, ultimately, an investment in their own honour and recognition. One of the more subtle temptations that we all have to fight against is the temptation to be self-serving in our self-giving. We are less likely to fall into this temptation if, like the widow, God remains the focus of our giving. Rather than giving to receive, we give because we have received; we give back to God out of what God has given to us.

By putting all she had to live on into the temple treasury, the vulnerable widow was making herself more vulnerable. It takes extraordinary trust in God to go out on a limb to the extent she did. Deep within her, she must have trusted that God would provide. In the first reading, another widow hesitated initially to share the little she and her son had with Elijah who had asked for something to eat and drink. She was vulnerable enough without making herself more vulnerable. Elijah assured her that if she shared the little she had, God would provide for her. It is in giving that she would receive.

This is the core of the gospel message: it is in giving that we receive, it is in dying that we are born to eternal life. 'Give and it will be given to you', Jesus says in Luke's gospel, 'A good measure, pressed down, shaken together, running over, will be put into your lap.' The giving Jesus refers to there is not only the giving of money. Our generous giving can take many forms. For some, it may take the form of forgiving someone who has done them wrong, for others it will be serving people with whatever gifts the Lord has given them. Whatever forms our giving takes, let both widows in today's readings be our teachers.

Thirty-Third Sunday in Ordinary Time

Most of us find endings difficult to deal with. We can find it hard to move on from something, especially if we have been reasonably happy where we have been. We can find transitions from one situation to a very different one difficult to manage, especially as we get older. Yet, we know from our experience that endings are an inevitable part of life. We cannot avoid change, including traumatic change. The best we can do is to try to manage change and the distress that change often brings us.

Some experiences of change are more distressing than others. There can be times in our lives when our whole world seems to change. This can be brought about by the onset of sudden illness or the death of a loved one or some event that forces us to literally change worlds. There can be huge distress involved in this for ourselves and for others. For a while we do not know where we are. We struggle to get our bearings.

It is this kind of cataclysmic change that today's readings seem to put before us. They speak of such a change not just as an individual experience but as a communal, indeed a cosmic, experience. We hear of the darkening of the sun and the shaking of the heavens, of a time of great distress, unparalleled since nations first came into existence. The readings seem to speak of an experience of ending that affects everybody in the most profound way. The language in which this profound and traumatic change is expressed is that of symbol and image, the language of the imagination.

Whenever we experience profound change that shakes the foundations of our world and that of others, we feel the need for some form of stability, something firm and fixed by which we can begin to navigate the strange territory in which we suddenly find ourselves. For most people such a solid point of reference will often take the form of another human being. A loved one, a friend, a family member who walks with us through the trauma, can keep us steady and enable us to negotiate the difficult journey on which we find ourselves. Whatever personal resources we have built up over our lives will stand to us in such times.

The readings of today's Mass remind us that our faith, our relationship with the Lord, can be an indispensable resource at such times. In the gospel reading, Jesus declares that: 'Heaven and earth will pass away, but my words will not pass away.' The Lord's words to us remain a constant in the midst of even the most traumatic and world-shattering experience of change. What is the Lord's word to us, in today's gospel reading? It is a word that assures us that the ending of the world, the ending of our own world, whatever form that might take, will always be accompanied by the coming of the Lord to us in power. The shaking of the heavens and the earth signals the Lord's coming to us with great power and glory. The Lord asks us to believe that he is present to us in the midst of the chaos that threatens to engulf us, and he asks us to trust that if we are open to his coming, to his presence, it is he who will gather us and not the chaos.

The gospel reading speaks of the Lord's coming using two quite different images. It says that he will come in the clouds with great power and glory and also that he is near, at the very gates. There is something of a contrast between the 'clouds' and the 'gates'. The 'clouds' suggest the otherness and the power of the Lord; the 'gates' suggest his nearness and his accessibility. In other words, the Lord's powerful coming at those moments of great trauma will not overwhelm us; it will be like meeting a good friend at the gate of our home. The old Irish saying comes to mind: 'God's help is nearer than the door.' Many people have found that their faith in the Lord's presence has helped to keep them going at times when they were suddenly thrust into strange and frightening territory.

When life is on an even keel, we have the opportunity to put in place resources that will stand to us when our world falls apart. In that sense, today, the day in which we find ourselves, is always the most important day of our lives. How we live today, what we value now, how we relate to the Lord and to other people in the present moment, is all laying a foundation for how we manage those earth shaking moments that come to us all.

Solemnity of Christ the King

We know from experience that those in authority are not always the people with the power. In an organisation the person who has been given the authority to lead can discover that the real power in the organisation belongs elsewhere, perhaps much further down the line.

The gospel reading today puts before us a meeting between two people, one who had been invested with great authority and another who had no authority at all. Pilate, as governor of Judea, had been entrusted with the authority of Caesar and worked to bring that authority to bear in a far-flung part of the Roman Empire. Jesus had no authority; he was without position or status, staring death by crucifixion in the face. Yet, of the two, it was Jesus who had the greater power. The influence of Jesus would turn out to be much more powerful than that of Pilate. Indeed, Pilate would have been no more than a footnote in history if Jesus had not been crucified on his watch.

The power of Jesus, as he stood before Pilate, was rooted in his intimate relationship with God. Jesus stands before Pilate as God incarnate, enfleshed Word. He alludes to this when he declares to Pilate that he has come into the world to bear witness to the truth. Jesus lived and died to bear witness to God in whom there is no falsehood. Jesus says of himself in John's gospel: 'I am the truth.' We could also say that Jesus came into the world to bear witness to love, to reveal God who is love. It is above all in laying down his life that Jesus reveals the God who is love.

Because Jesus was truth incarnate and love incarnate, he had great power, even as he appeared helpless before Pilate. Jesus' power was not an oppressive power, but a liberating and life-giving power. He embodied the truth that sets free and gave expression to the love that brings life. We, his disciples, are called to be powerful in the sense in which Jesus was powerful. Jesus says to Pilate: 'All who are on the side of truth listen to my voice.' 'Those who listen to his voice', his disciples, are those who are on the side of truth, on the side of love. We show ourselves to be the Lord's disciples by being truthful as Jesus was truthful, by loving as Jesus loved. Truth and love are two facets of God, and when we are truthful and loving people we show ourselves to be people of God, revealers of God as Jesus was, powerful in the way he was.

We are to hold together in our lives both the value of truth and the value of love, especially in the way we relate to people. Truth without love can be hard and harsh. If we truly care for people, we will only give them as much truth as they are capable of hearing at the time. Similarly, love without a commitment to truth can become overly indulgent. Loving others can mean at times helping them to see something that they need to see but have become blind to. The letter to the Ephesians states: 'Speaking the truth in love, we must grow up in every way into him who is the head, into Christ.' Because Christ was the perfect expression of truth and love, whenever we live truthful and loving lives we grow up into Christ. Growing up into Christ is a calling that engages us for the whole of our earthly lives. It is only in the next life that we will grow fully into Christ.

Today's feast calls on us to grow as disciples of Christ the King by bearing witness to the way of truth and love that Jesus embodied. Today's second reading speaks of Jesus as the faithful witness. He witnessed faithfully to the God who sent him into the world, to truth and to love. He lived in this world but he bore witness to God's world, to the values of God's kingdom. His faithful witness often brought him into conflict with those in authority, like Pilate.

We too are called to be faithful witnesses as Jesus was. Like Jesus we are immersed in this world; we are children of our present-day culture and, yet, we are called to witness to God's world. We are to witness to the values of God's kingdom even as we live under various forms of earthly authority. We are to be truthful in a world where secrecy and deceit can be rampant; we are to be self-giving in a world that often promotes self-serving. This will often mean taking the more difficult path, as it did for Jesus. Yet, we have his assurance that his path is the path of life.

The Birth of John the Baptist

Within the church we do not normally celebrate the birthday of a saint. Feast days of saints are generally on the day of their death. John the Baptist is the only saint, after Jesus himself, whose birth the church celebrates with a solemn feast. We celebrate the birth of John the Baptist on 24 June, six months before we celebrate the birth of Jesus on 25 December. According to Luke's gospel, the birth of John was announced to Zechariah, John's father, six months before the birth of Jesus was announced to Mary, Jesus' mother. The celebration of the birth of Jesus at Christmas coincides more or less with the winter solstice. Just as the light of the sun begins to make a comeback after darkness has reached its peak, we celebrate the birth of the light of the world. The celebration of the birth of John the Baptist coincides, in contrast, with the summer solstice. Just as the light of the sun begins to decrease, after reaching its peak, we celebrate the birth of the one who said, Jesus 'must increase, but I must decrease'.

There was something special about John the Baptist. The gospel reading this morning suggests that his being given the name 'John' was itself special. In those days children were generally named after their parents or grandparents or some other family member. In the case of John the Baptist, this convention went out the window. John's parents understood that God wanted their child to be called 'John'. Neighbours and relations objected to this name: 'No one in your family has that name.' However, God's way of working does not always follow convention. God was about to do something new through this child. God wanted him to be called John, a name which in Hebrew means 'the Lord has shown favour', because God was inaugurating a new era of favour through John. The neighbours and relations meant well but, without realising it, they were hindering what God was about to do. This is a failing that we are all prone to. Our conventional way of doing things can sometimes be a hindrance to what God wants to do. Today's second reading refers to God's 'whole purpose'. Our preferences and plans can be very small in comparison to God's whole purpose. Our allegiance to family conventions, or even to certain church conventions, can sometimes get in the way of God's whole purpose for our lives.

After the resistance of the neighbours and relations had been overcome, they went on to ask: 'What will this child turn out to be?' They sensed that something bigger was afoot here than what they had expected. They began to see that this child's future would not conform to the conventions they took for granted. The adult John resisted the temptation to become what others wanted him to be. According to today's second reading, he declared: 'I am not the one you imagine me to be.' Rather, he turned out to be the person God wanted him to be and that is why Jesus would go on to say: 'Among those born of women no one is greater than John.' John was great because he was faithful to God's whole purpose for his life. He was faithful to God's call, faithful unto death.

The question that the neighbours and relations ask of John, 'What will this child turn out to be?' could be asked of any of us, not just when we are infants but at every stage of our lives, 'What will we turn out to be?', or to put the question in other terms, 'Who is God calling us to be'? 'What name is God giving to us?' Our calling is to surrender to God's 'whole purpose' for our lives, as John did. God's purpose for John's life and God's purpose for all our lives are the same. God wants all of us to do what John did, to point out the Saviour, to make way for Jesus, to lead others to him by what we say and do. Our struggle to be faithful to this purpose of God for our lives will often mean going against the conventional way of doing things. It will often lead us down the road less travelled. It may leave neighbours and friends scratching their heads in puzzlement.

John the Baptist, whose birth we celebrate today, has something to teach us about how we might keep faithful to this God-given calling. He was a man of the desert, a man of prayer. We all need to find our own desert place of prayer if we are to remain true to our calling, if we are to be faithful to God's whole purpose for our lives, if we are to turn out as God wants us to.

The Dedication of the Lateran Basilica

In the early fourth century the first Christian emperor, Constantine, had a church built on land that once belonged to the Laterani family. That church of Constantine was the precursor of the present Lateran Basilica. The Baptistery building attached to the present Basilica is where Constantine was baptised. This Basilica is now the Cathedral church of the Diocese of Rome. It is the church of the Pope in his capacity as Bishop of Rome. For that reason, it has the title, 'mother and head of all the churches of the world'.

The day when that great Basilica was first consecrated to God might bring to mind for us the day when our own parish church was consecrated. Any church building, be it the Basilica of John Lateran or the local parish church, is a monument to the faith of many people. Today we remember those whose faith helped to build this parish church. Every church building tells a story about the faith community who gather in the building. In that sense today's feast is less about a church building and more about the people we call church. Paul's words to the Corinthians this morning are addressed to every parish community: 'You are God's building.' For Paul, the local faith community is the Temple of God, where God's Spirit is dwelling. This church building is most itself when it is filled with the people who are the church.

Every parish community needs to attend to the fabric of the church building but, more importantly, it needs to attend to its own faith life. As a parish community, we need to keep our church building in good condition, and we also need to live out our baptism more fully. When our faith is vibrant, our church buildings will be alive. Any parish community has only limited financial resources, and important decisions have to be made as to how much of those resources go towards the upkeep of the building and how much go towards the nurturing of the faith community. Priority must always be given to the believing community for whom the building exists. Paul in that second reading reminds us that the foundation of the believing community is Jesus Christ. As individual believers and as a community of faith we are called to build our lives on the person of Jesus, by keeping ourselves open to his Spirit. That is our shared baptismal calling. In attending to that calling we give meaning to the building in which we gather.

Although the parish community comes before the parish church building, every parish community needs a sacred space where they can gather and where they are helped to focus on the Lord. Most of us feel the need of a place apart, where we can respond to the Lord's presence in worship. A church like this is such a place apart. It is not a place where we live or work or recreate. When we enter a church building, we cross a kind of a threshold, passing over from the space in which we live, work and recreate into a different kind of space, a space that, hopefully, helps us to pray, and that enables us to look a little deeper, so that we come to recognise the Lord in whom we live and move and have our being. A sacred space, such as a church building, is a place where we come apart – at times to be alone but, more often, to be with other members of the parish community. It is a place where we are reminded that we do not travel the path of faith alone, but always with other believers, fellow travellers on the pilgrimage of life. It is a place where we experience the Lord's presence in each other, as well as in the Eucharist and in the other sacraments. If it helps us to experience the Lord's presence, our church building, like the Temple in Ezekiel's vision in the first reading, will be a life-giving place, a place where we will be refreshed and renewed in spirit, mind, heart and body.

The gospel reading reminds us, however, that even sacred spaces, like the Temple in Jerusalem, can cease to serve their intended purpose. Jesus declared that his Father's house had been turned into a market. A church building has the potential to be a well-spring of life and hope for the parish community. If it is to realise that potential, we need to pay attention to what goes on there. As a parish community we need to keep working on our sacred space so that it remains a place that helps us to be more open to the Spirit of God living among us, a place that empowers us to become God's temple in the world.

Feast of Saints Peter and Paul

We often struggle to get to know each other well. If we were to ask even a close friend: 'Who do you say I am?' they might find it difficult to give an adequate answer to that question. If people are to know us, we need to reveal ourselves to them, and self-revelation does not come easy to us, even when we are in the presence of those who love us.

The gospels suggest that people struggled to get to know Jesus. When Jesus turns to his disciples in today's gospel reading and asks them: 'Who do people say the Son of Man is?' the answer to his question showed that the general perception of him was somewhat inadequate. Jesus was not John the Baptist, or Elijah, or Jeremiah, or one of the other prophets, even though he had something in common with all of them. When Jesus asked his disciples the more probing question: 'But you, who do you say that I am?' Peter's answer on behalf of the others was much more satisfactory: 'You are the Christ, the Son of the living God.' Here indeed was real insight into Jesus' identity. However, Jesus immediately declares that this insight of Peter was God-given; it was not simply the result of Peter's own natural abilities. If any of us are to come to know Jesus more fully, it is only with God's help that we can do this; we need the light of God's Spirit if we are to come to know God's Son.

Today we celebrate the feast of Saints Peter and Paul. According to the gospel reading, what singled Peter out from the other disciples was his God-given insight into the identity of Jesus. It is because of his unique insight that Jesus gives Peter a unique role among his followers. He is to be the firm foundation, on which Jesus will build his church. Peter's role is further spelt out by Jesus giving him the keys of the kingdom of heaven. The image of the keys suggests authority. The nature of that authority is expressed in terms of binding and loosing. This is probably a reference to a teaching authority. Peter is being entrusted with the task of authoritatively interpreting the teaching of Jesus for other members of the church. Later on in the gospel Jesus will criticise the Pharisees for locking people out of the kingdom of God by their teaching. In contrast, Peter's teaching should pave the way for people to enter God's kingdom. All

Christians can look to Peter as the one to whom Jesus entrusted his own teaching role in a special way. He is the patron of all teachers of the faith. Peter reminds us that authoritative teaching is grounded in insight into the person of Jesus. We need to know Jesus well if our teaching is to be true to his.

What about Paul, that other saint whose feast we celebrate today? If the gospel reading associates teaching with Peter, the second reading associates preaching with Paul. In that reading Paul refers to the Lord who 'gave me power, so that through me the whole message might be preached for all the pagans to hear'. Paul was the great preacher of the gospel to the pagans. He preached it for the last time in the city of Rome where, like Peter, he died for his faith in Christ, during the persecution of the church under the emperor Nero. The extract from his second letter to Timothy that is our second reading today may well have been written from his Roman imprisonment: 'I have fought the good fight to the end; I have run the race to the finish; I have kept the faith.' The image of the fight and the race suggest that 'keeping the faith' was a struggle; it did not come easy to him. Keeping the faith does not always come easy to us, either. In all kinds of ways, our life experience can work to undermine our faith in the Lord. We might learn to look to Paul as someone who can be an inspiration to us in our own keeping of the faith. Paul was very aware that keeping the faith was not due primarily to his own efforts; it was the Lord who enabled him to keep the faith. As he says in that reading: 'The Lord stood by me and gave me power.' It is the Lord who empowers all of us to keep the faith; his faithfulness to us enables us to be faithful to him. As Paul wrote a little earlier in that same second letter to Timothy: 'If we are faithless, we remain faithful.'

Feast of the Presentation

A blessing for any parish is to have a group of parishioners who work together to serve the needs of the senior members of the community. The generosity and commitment of such people can ensure that older people in the parish are offered a whole range of activities that they can choose from.

There is a very good example of an active older person in today's gospel reading. Anna, the daughter of Phanuel, was an eighty-four year old woman. The gospel reading tells us that she was serving God night and day, with fasting and prayer. She was also something of a preacher because she spoke of the child Jesus to all who looked forward to the deliverance of Jerusalem. She certainly qualifies as one of the active aged. Simeon was elderly too. He had been waiting a long time to see the Christ, and having seen him he was now ready to depart this life. He was a regular visitor to the Temple, going wherever the Holy Spirit led him. Here was another active, aged person. He was also someone who was alert to the deeper meaning of things. He recognised the true significance of the child that was brought into the temple by the young couple Mary and Joseph.

The gospel reading puts before us a meeting between youth and age. A very young couple with their child enter the Temple of God where they meet a much older man and woman. This meeting turned out to be a source of blessing for both generations. Youth was graced by age, and age was graced by youth. This can be true of our own experience as well. The younger generation can be a source of great blessing to the older generation, and *vice versa*. They each have something to give the other. The promise of youth can be an inspiration to older people. The experience and wisdom of age can serve as a source of strength and stability for the young. We need to bring the generations into contact with each other, because each has something to offer to the other. The generation in the middle are often best placed to bring these two generations together. I remember when I was a child my father bringing me and my brothers to see my grandparents every Sunday morning. Those visits had some kind of worthwhile influence on me that is hard to define. You could say that I was blessed and graced by those visits.

No matter what generation we belong to, our calling as followers of the Lord is to bless and grace others by our presence. All of the people who met in the Temple in today's gospel reading were the better for that meeting – Mary, Joseph, Simeon, Anna and even the child Jesus himself. It might prompt any one of us to ask the question: 'Are others the better for having met me?' The second reading this morning mentions two qualities that the adult Jesus had. He is described there as a 'compassionate and trustworthy high priest'. Because he was compassionate and trustworthy, people from all walks of life were the better for having met him. The presence of these qualities in our own lives will make us a source of blessing for others. A compassionate person is someone who, in some way, can enter into, or tries to enter into, our experience of life, someone who can feel with us and for us. A trustworthy person is someone who honours and respects whatever we might entrust to him or her. They can be relied upon to hold in trust whatever we give them of ourselves. These are qualities that, in a sense, are of God. They are the fruit of the Holy Spirit. They are found in those who, like Simeon, are open to the Holy Spirit.

Jesus has these qualities to a unique degree. He is compassionate towards us because he has shared the same flesh and blood we all share, as the second reading reminds us. He has become completely like us, having been tempted in every way that we are. He is trustworthy. Having given his life for us on the cross, he has shown that he was worthy of our trust. This compassionate and trustworthy high priest enters the temple of our lives every day, as he entered the temple in Jerusalem. He enters our lives in a special way through the Eucharist that we are now celebrating. We are invited to welcome him as Simeon and Anna welcomed him – with an open heart, in a spirit of praise and thanksgiving. In receiving the Lord's coming in this way, we will be blessed, his Spirit will be renewed in us, and we will become a source of blessing for others.

Feast of the Transfiguration

Many people like being up the hills and mountains. There is something about being on a height which we can find exhilarating and exciting. It feels different up there. You are somehow above it all. You have a different perspective.

Peter, James and John made their living from the sea. They were fishermen who must have spent long hours on the Sea of Galilee or by its shores. In this morning's gospel reading, Jesus takes them away from the sea, up a high mountain. There, on that mountain, they had a memorable experience. They saw Jesus as they had never seen him before, transfigured, his clothes dazzling white. As Peter says in today's second reading: 'We saw his majesty for ourselves.' In an earlier chapter of his gospel, Mark had described Jesus and his disciples in a storm at sea, the boat battling against the wind and waves. Now on the mountain, the storm must have seemed a distant memory as they were absorbed by an experience of Jesus that made Peter cry out: 'It is wonderful for us to be here.' The hell of the storm had given way to this heavenly experience on the mountain. Yet, an even more hellish storm lay ahead for the disciples. They would soon come down the mountain and continue the journey towards Jerusalem, the city where they would experience suffering, death and failure.

In our own lives we will probably have experienced both the storm at sea and the peace of the mountain top. When we look back on our lives, the more painful experiences can sometimes stand out more. Hopefully, we will also remember times when, like Peter, we said: 'It is wonderful to be here.' These were times when we felt deeply happy and at peace, when we sensed God's presence in a special way. The gospel reading this morning invites us to remember those moments and to continue to draw life from them.

I am struck by that little word 'here' in Peter's statement: 'It is wonderful for us to be here.' So often we can find ourselves wishing that we were somewhere else, not 'here', but 'there'. We image that we would be happier if we were in a different place, with different people, doing different things. In some instances that can be the case. It can be important at times for people to

144

move, because where they are is anything but wonderful. But at other times, our wishing to be somewhere else can come from our failure to appreciate where we are, the people around us now. Maybe if we saw more deeply, we would appreciate more fully the here and the now, and we might find ourselves saying more often: 'It is good to be here.'

On the mountain top, Peter, James and John saw Jesus more deeply than they had ever seen him before. They were captivated by the mystery of his identity: 'This is my Son, the beloved.' They saw that there was more to him than they had realised. So often, there is more to the place we are in, and to the people we are with, than we realise. Sometimes our way of seeing where we are and who we are with can be very restricted. We can miss something important about the 'here' and the 'now'. In one of our acclamations at Mass, we proclaim, 'Heaven and earth are full of your glory.' We acknowledge in that acclamation how the created world is charged with God's presence. That is especially true with regard to the human person who alone is made in the very image of God. God could say of each person we meet: 'This is my beloved.' As God invited the disciples on the mountain to see Jesus more deeply, he invites us to see each other more deeply, to relate to each other in a way that acknowledges the wonder of our being. We can fail to appreciate what is all around us. God calls us to cherish and celebrate the wonder of life all around us, as the disciples celebrated the wonder of Jesus on the mountain.

We are also called to allow the wonder of our being to shine forth to full effect. In the second reading, St Peter speaks of God's word as a lamp that lightens our way. If we pay attention to that word, he says, the morning star will rise in our minds. In other words, we will be filled with the Lord's own light. Something of the light that so enthralled the disciples on the mountain will shine through us. It is in paying attention to the Lord present in his word, in listening to him and allowing his word to shape our lives, that the wonder of our being becomes more evident to all.

The Triumph of the Cross

The words 'triumph' and 'cross' do not normally belong together. 'Triumph' suggests celebration, achievement, recognition. 'Cross' indicates suffering, humiliation, defeat. The association of triumph and cross is all the stranger when we consider that 'cross', in this case, refers to the act of crucifixion, the most painful and degrading form of punishment that the Roman Empire could devise. How could any one who ended up cruci-fied ever be said to have triumphed? It is hard to think of a greater paradox that the phrase 'the triumph of the cross'.

Yet, as Christians, we don't find that phrase in any way strange. We know what it means. Indeed, within thirty years of the crucifixion of Jesus by the Romans, the first and perhaps the greatest Christian theologian, St Paul, writing to the small Christian community in the city of Corinth, stated: 'We preach Christ crucified ... Christ the power of God and the wisdom of God.' Christ crucified – the power and the wisdom of God. Perhaps no one in the history of Christianity has expressed the paradox of the triumph of the cross more eloquently than that.

What is this power that shows itself in such degrading weak-ness? It is the power of love, the power of a love that is greater than any human love, the love spoken about in today's gospel reading. 'God so loved the world that he gave his only Son.' Here was a divine love that became a human love in the life and death of Jesus, a love so powerful that it was in no way dimin-ished by the experience of rejection and hatred.

Our own ability to love is very influenced by the extent to which our love is returned. Our most creative energies can be drained out of us by negative experiences of others. It is not so with God. On the cross, Jesus revealed a love so powerful that that it extended even to those who brought about his death; in his dying he demonstrated a love that triumphed over all the forces that tried to crush it. This is why we speak of the triumph of the cross. As the Preface of today's Mass says: 'The tree of de-feat became the tree of victory.'

We continue to venerate the cross today because we know that the triumph of that Good Friday is a triumph in which we all share. The light that shone in that awful darkness continues to shine on all of us. The love that burst forth from the hill of Golgotha continues to flow into all our lives. In particular, the Eucharist that we celebrate makes the triumph of the cross present to us today. God so loves the world that he continues to give us his Son. As St Paul puts it: 'As often as you eat this bread and drink this cup, you proclaim the Lord's death until he comes.' Every time we gather to celebrate the Eucharist, we proclaim the triumph of the Lord's death, the triumph of a greater love, and in and through our proclamation we are taken up into that triumph. We continue to be drawn by a love that is not in any way diminished by our lack of response to it, by our many failings and weaknesses. The Eucharist has been described as bread broken for a broken people, or to put it another way, love given to a sinful people.

Not only are we the beneficiaries of the triumph of God's love on Calvary, the triumph of the cross, but sometimes our own lives can reveal to others the triumph of the cross. The triumph of the cross can show itself in our lives in all kinds of simple, non-dramatic ways. It reveals itself in the tolerance and humour we show to each other against all the odds, in the willingness to let go of old hurts, in the refusal to play the game of tit for tat. It shows itself in the bearing of terminal illness with patience and dignity, in the fidelity to significant commitments when they become costly, in the loving service that endures even when it is not appreciated. The triumph of the cross was powerfully present in the words of a Catholic taxi-driver some years ago in the North of Ireland as he stood by the grave of his murdered son: 'I forgive those who killed my son and I say to them: bury your hatred in his grave. Bury your hatred as I bury my son.' We might pray on this feast that the triumph of the cross would continue to take flesh in our lives, so that the life-giving power that flowed from the side of the crucified Christ might continue to flow out through all our lives.